Part I

STORIES AND RECIPES
OF THE GREAT DEPRESSION
of the 1930's

Compiled by Rita Van Amber

Part II

MORE FROM YOUR KITCHEN TODAY
(Begins on page 175)

Compiled by Janet Van Amber Paske
Home Economist

THE WAY IT WAS

This compilation is a documentary of the experiences
and domestic history of the Great Depression of the
1930s. The time is right for it to be recorded,
before it is forgotten. Children, already, don't
quite believe it, which is not surprising. This
country has changed so dramatically in the past 50
years it is hard to believe we were in such desperate
straights so recently.

The present generation cannot begin to understand the
strange changes which went through our country at that
time; it was a turning point in history.

First banks became worthless. Then businesses and
factories closed their doors one after the other
when consumer-buying came to a virtual standstill.
Farm prices had dropped out of sight and jobs became
nonexistent. There was no money flow. The structure
of American society had disintegrated.

Unfortunately, the stories one hears about those times.
are true...we know they are. Our large population of
Senior Citizens is that generation, and they remember
all too vividly the experiences of that decade of
poverty. It was a time when the middle class was
reduced to being poor. We had only two classes, the
haves and the have-nots.

You are a survivor of the Great Depression if these
little ditties ring a bell in your memory: mairzy
doats and dosey doats and little lambs eat ivy; or
the three little fiddies and a mama fiddy too, fim
said the mama fiddy, fim if you can. The latter
reminding us of mothers giving pep talks to their
children as they went out into the world into a
jobless society. People found something to laugh
at with the arrival of the light-hearted songs and
lyrics.

Then adorable Shirley Temple made her appearance when

we needed someone to take the gloom off our daily
lives. About this time the Walt Disney characters
became popular. Mortimer Mouse soon became a
favorite. His name was changed to Mickey and they
loved him more.

But nothing delighted that generation more than
when Mama Dione delivered five little look-alike
baby girls. National and world fame was bestowed
upon the Doctor and Papa Dione who vied intensely
for top honors. Mama Dione was seldom mentioned.

And of course, "Kilroy was here". All would be well
where Kilroy had been. He left his message on the
walls, everywhere. Eventually he followed the men
overseas to fight a war, but in the meantime he was
here, standing by.

It is all a part of the American experience. It is
a reflection of the times in the bleak 1930s, and
this book is intended as a recording to be sure
parents are recognized for their historical
endurance.

It was time to dredge up memories of those days
while many of the real survivors, the parents,
are still here. The mothers who cooked those meals
out of nothing and made them taste so good and the
fathers who worked harder than ever, in a futile
attempt to keep things as they were before, and not
to admit failure.

They were a proud people, and they passed that
virtue on to the next generation, our Senior
Citizens of today. Families in those days didn't
want to admit that times were hard around their
place.

Survival tactics taught the children early to dig
deep to find the best in themselves. They had to
succeed, to perform - it was sink or swim.

For the girls, they were right at their mother's

side observing and learning her ingenuity as a way of life. As a result of the constant need the women became near magicians in their large kitchens, out-performing in putting meals on the table. They improvised warm clothing for the family to sustain them through bitter cold winters where children often walked miles to school.

Grandma's old shredded nightgown became baby clothing and lining for mittens, while Grandpa's old absolutely worn out socks became long, warm cuffs for those mittens. All old clothing was carefully recycled and all bits and pieces were put to good use.

Is it any wonder that the children of this school of life-long lessons grew up to value their possessions and their incomes? They became a frugal society. Waste was a severe taboo, for fear they would be in need again. While the memory of the poverty years were never to be erased, the lessons learned were generally permanent. Security became a life-long aim.

Our Senior Citizens have every right to be proud of their accomplishments. They pulled our country through World War II and they kept the fighting from our shores. And when they came back they built this country up again from the convalescence of the poverty years and of the war efforts. They didn't stop there; they built other needy countries up as well and put them on their feet. And now this same large population of citizens continue to protect our economy by pouring the dollars they saved into consumer buying, supporting our system from faltering when recessions occur.

This is not a bad record for kids who had to put fresh cardboard in the soles of their shoes every morning to keep from wearing their socks out. They only had one set of underwear which had to be washed every evening and hung over the warming oven to dry for the next morning's school.

But, the SALUTE goes to the parents, our elderly now,

who weathered the long storm as young men and women.
They had the same rosy dream of a bright future
everyone begins their young lives with. Their's was
the "epitaph of shattered dreams", as they called
that decade.

While those parents made the best of a bad situation,
they still kept their standards high and taught their
children strong values, passing on a priceless
heritage.

ISBN 0-9619663-1-9

TABLE OF CONTENTS

Part I

Recipes from the Great Depression

Part II

More From Your Kitchen Today

MY FAMILY HERITAGE OF RECOLLECTIONS AND
HAPPENINGS OF THE 1930s.

Date Recorded_____

YOU NEED THIS COOKBOOK IF:

YOU ARE A GRANDMOTHER and wish to have your children and grandchildren know how you lived and survived in the nation's greatest crisis, the Great Depression of the 1930's, the drought, the locust invasion and more.

A DOCTOR HAS TOLD YOU OR A MEMBER OF YOUR FAMILY not to consume foods containing preservatives or food colors (asthma, allergies, cancer, behavioral and learning problems and stress control).

YOU ARE SHORT OF CASH and need money to make that rent or car payment (new clothes, vacation, savings) while dining on delicious wholesome meals.

WEIGHT LOSING DIET WHILE YOU SAVE MONEY: You should not have to PAY to lose weight. The reward should be all yours, right in your own pocket. The vegetable soups once a day provide a satisfying and nutritious way to lose weight gradually and continuously. A large bowl with dumplings for lunch, fruit and a piece of toast, preferably whole wheat, for breakfast, plus a modest size dinner consisting of protein, vegetables, potato and salad will keep most people well satisfied. Two glasses of skim milk for lunches rounds out the nutrition with one multi-vitamin tablet a day. If you need a snack, an apple or low-cal soda can be enjoyed, but no alcoholic beverages.

1

```
EAT IT UP
          WEAR IT OUT
     MAKE IT DO
          OR DO WITHOUT
```

A favorite patriotic 1930's Great
Depression motto used by people to pacify
themselves when they had to forego
necessities.

THANK YOU

The biblical quotation, "Ask and you shall receive," surely held true for me. I received an awesome response from the "Lifestyles" newspaper article in the Eau Claire Leader-Telegram by Karen Harder requesting recipes, anecdotes and stories of the Great Depression of the 1930's. Such graciousness is almost unbelievable. They all encouraged me by mail, phone and in person to continue on with my venture, and many thanked me for the opportunity to contribute something they felt should be preserved in a book.

The initial encouragement came from Dr. Carl Haywood, the University of Wisconsin—Eau Claire and Karen Harder for the push I needed to make this project a reality.

To all the generous people who contributed in one way or another, I extend my sincerest gratitude. Any material I did not find room for will be used in a later printing.

The letters, phone calls and visits have brought back memories to all of us of our nation's longest and hardest national disaster, as it was lived in this midwest area.

We have learned that our personal experiences in striving to make the best of it have taught us dependability, self-reliance, awareness of the needs of others and money management. Although we lost a part of our childhood by having to help out, the deprivation of enjoyment matured us as children beyond our age.

We also more fully understand the role of our mothers, who were young women who worked unbearably hard to somehow manage to provide their men and children with the most basic needs in food and home management.

The ingenuity they were called upon to use was sometimes almost super human achievement.

Our mothers demonstrated a positive role in dealing with their plight and in solving problems. And they were successful. They kept their families together and they taught their children values which became our greatest assets for the difficult forthcoming World War II years and ultimately to build America up again.

Rita C. Van Amber

3

Dedication

This book is dedicated to my Mother and to all the mothers who so valiantly struggled through the Great Depression in their kitchens to keep body and soul of their families together.

Rita Van Amber

STORIES AND ANECDOTES FROM THE DEPRESSION

During the 30's, which were some of the most difficult times in recorded history, there was little cash, especially for the farmers or anyone in a like situation. My mother used to pride herself on trading in her eggs for an equal amount of groceries, seldom if ever, having to come up with any cash.

As I grew older, I appreciate more than ever, the difficult times she must have encountered, trying to make ends meet.

Paying for a farm during a depression, as well as dust dry years, would serve as a hard task master for the very hardiest.

She used to tell me that one of her lowest points, was when she had to can (preserve) weeds. The garden didn't do well at all during the driest time, but the weeds, lamb's quarters, still flourished, so she canned them, for something on the cellar shelves against the winter coming on.

We must have eaten a lot of lamb's quarters in those hard years. Yet she was such an innovative cook that to this day I still love those greens.

My husband had eaten dandelion greens as a kid in those same dreadful years, but had never heard of eating lamb's quarters, which are much more mellow. But he came to relish them, and now each spring reminds me to hunt for some for a meal.

He also tells me that one year during the 30's there were no presents for Christmas for lack of money, and he spent a sad Christmas eve entertaining himself cutting pictures from old magazines. I could cry at the thought. I guess my parents had more imagination, for we perhaps were poorer than that, but for one of my most memorable Christmases I received a tiny cupboard made from three wooden cheese boxes, and inside the little shelves were doll dresses my mother cut out for me to sew together by hand.

Just by that little gesture alone, she wisely gave me something to do, rather than sew them herself, thereby stretching out Christmas a little more.

(Continued)

5

(Continued)

I never really knew we were poor. My mother had original
ideas both in cooking and in sewing, that I wasn't aware
that we ever went without. Oh, the difference in "making
do" and making a "to do" in what you don't have. A positive attitude made all the difference in your outlook.

As a result of her maintaining a balanced diet of foods
she could magically make taste so good, my brothers and
myself have for the most part, maintained healthy bodies
all these years. We've never had a broken bone, never
been seriously ill. And a good share of our good fortune,
I'm certain, is due, in part to wise imaginative parents,
who did their very best to bring us through unscathed, the
bleakest years in history.

Anonymous
Menomonie WI

***

In all of this, I have one most important duty, that my
family grows up with the best possible nourishment I can
provide. Our health must come first.

H. Cichy
Millerville MN

***

In 1934, west of Port Wing, 100 acres of Lake Superior
Lake Shore was for sale for $100.

Most everyone else, including Shirley T. of Menomonie,
didn't buy it because it was too speculative. Even though
he found a job and was earning $1.00 a day, his money was
too hard to come by to take the chance. Futhermore, it
was all he had to live on and he went all the way to the
sugar beet fields of Iowa to get the job.

***

"I worked for my room and board for an old farmer in North
Dakota. He was getting so old and farms didn't sell, he
wanted to give it to me, stock, machinery and all. I
turned him down."

John S.
North Carolina

6

"I gave the preacher my last dollar after he married us. Our plans had been to go to St. Paul on the train for our honeymoon. I was really sweating it that day wondering how I was going to do it. Then my uncle gave me $20.00 as a wedding gift."

Chuck Vasey
Menomonie, WI

"Yes! they were "heart breaking years" to remember, from World War I hardships and World War II economy cooking".

Linda Weber

"The Depression was a good education."

Virginia Fyksen
Eau Claire, WI

"My parents were middle class farmers when they started. Then the depression came and it changed all that. We wore our shoes out with big holes in the soles so we'd put fresh cardboard in every morning before leaving for school.

"We all wore the same dresses at school. They were made out of feed bags and only one neighbor had a pattern. So we all used the same pattern with the same rickrack around the neck, sleeves and hems".

Gwen Manske
Menomonie, WI

The gas tank was getting low and we couldn't make it up the steep hill in the Model T so we turned it around right there and backed it up all the way. Gravity-feed gas tanks were under the front seat.

We coasted down every hill so the gas would take us there and back. It was 19 cents a gallon.

Soda pop was 5 cents a bottle and it was real genuine grape. We never got any.

George

7

Known as the decade of hard times, the 1930's was marked by the drama and chaos of the worst economic depression in history.

Every family knew what it was to live on bread and Wisconsin gravy.

Delores Harris
Eau Claire, WI

"The Lord always saw us through and we never wasted anything".

Lois Ball
Augusta, WI

Young men came up from the cities to work for their room and board at my fathers farm.

Our farm had a hard pan so the drought affected us less than neighboring counties. This soil condition held moisture in the ground longer.

Clark County

Vinegar, King of the Cupboard

Since Bibical times women have known what a touch of vinegar would do for food. Caesar's legions glubbed drinking water laced with it. Uses range from preservatives to deodorants in a room or a fishy fry pan.

Vinegar keeps apples from turning brown, it is a meat tenderizer, and a dash of it in bread and rolls makes them delightfully crusty. A tablespoon full used in place of cream of tartar in meringue makes it beautifully high. And yes! Grandmother stirred up a vinegar pie that was equal to any lemon concoction.

A cloth dipped in vinegar and then in salt easily takes tarnish off old brass or copper, while boiled vinegar and water kept lime deposit from forming on the inside of the tea

(Continued)

kettle. Three tablespoons of vinegar to a quart of water takes stains out of carpets. Vinegar with it's myriad of uses truly is King of the Cupboard.

Submitted by   Phyliss Schroeder
                                Cedar Falls, WI

Everything was very inexpensive, but no one had any cash flow with which to buy it.

A spool of cotton thread cost 5 cents. A lot of it was needed to sew all those feed bags into wearing apparel and bedding. The bags came in a variety of printed patterns so more than one could be purchase when making clothes for adults or for quilts or other bedding.

We had sheep so we always had wool batts for quilt making, combined with the all cotton feed bags, we had good quilts.

Helen C.
Millerville, MN

"I took my baby along to work at the Lucas Cheese factory. He played and slept in a playpen all day long. I'd go over now and then when he fussed to tend to him, but not for long. I was being paid $1.75 a week to work full days and I was fortunate to have a job."

Erlenne McColpin
Menomonie, WI

Many households were so strapped for cash that all cream had to be sold and none used for meals. Eileen Hyman of Eau Claire, WI, remembers looking forward to a very special treat on Sundays. Her father allowed using cream skimmed off the milk to be used that day.

Jeepers Creepers, cigarette smoking was in and so was roller skating.

* * *

Our pin curls bounced as we danced the Jitterbug but the Matron tapped us on the shoulder if our knees showed just a little bit.

* * *

Riding the Rails and Locusts

There was an explosion of young displaced men riding the rails in pursuit of jobs. Any jobs, even if only for board.

They couldn't eat at Dad's table. There wasn't enough to go around and there were younger ones to feed.

The drought had just about destroyed Dad. He had a bit of marsh hay until the locusts came. You could hear them coming. Like the core of a frightening storm, a steady ominous hum getting louder.

We all ran for the cattle and put them in the barn. We took the dog inside too. One horse got wild and ran away. The locusts ate his eyes out.

My Dad drove twenty miles north on 64 sliding on the road of mashed grasshoppers to give the alarm. They set a wide back fire and got a lot of them.

But nothing was left. These things were three inches long and even damaged the potatoes, turnips and carrots in the ground. They were a thick heavy coat where they slammed against the barn.

It left us with nothing. It hurt me to see Dad so utterly defeated and crushed.

Wheeler, WI

"I can still remember all the good meals mother used to make even though times were hard".

Dartha Sell
Osseo, WI

"We were married in 1933 and our furniture was mostly orange crates. But believe we were more happy and had more love than today".

Phyllis Schroeder
Menomonie, WI

* * *

"We had the cellar full of canned goods and vegetables, we didn't go to the store for every meal. Maybe once or twice a month".

Phyllis Schroeder
Menomonie, WI

* * *

"Good old days would kill off this generation in a weeks time".

* * *

"I talked with this nice old man and asked him if he never drove the car in the winter since he had no rust on it. He said he drove it all the time for years and years, but he washes it in fall with a cup of fuel oil in the water to prevent salt damage".

Judy Hendricks
Menomonie, WI

* * *

Raisins were 5 cents a 1b. But you seldom had the 5 cents.

H.C.

Double dip ice cream cones were 5 cents each but you didn't have the nickel.

Butternuts were for the picking if you were smarter than the squirrel.

R.V.
Menomonie, WI

As a girl I remember carrying a glass can of cooked oatmeal to school and the teacher put it in a dish pan of hot water.

And how we waited for the rhubarb to peak thru the snow - our spring tonic Mother always said.

We sold our best Gurnsey cow for $27.00 to pay a feed bill at the mill.

Somehow I do not care for sorghum now.

Life was simple, friends and neighbors cared about one another.

Vera Lindsay
Mondovi, WI

Nothing was thrown away - we ate what was fixed. We never said "yuk" about food or we would have been disciplined.

Alma Smith
Woodville, WI

I sewed my 4th of July dance dress out of white cotton with red polka dots. My good looking cousin Louie taught me to dance to the Blue Skirt Waltz and the Schottische.

The Wardrobe

All discarded old clothing was recycled into new items. The seams were carefully ripped apart and the pieces washed, ironed and the basic pattern was used on the reverse side. This side was always colorful and looked like new. The basic pattern was used for everything. Generally cut out of newspaper, you made your own changes to suit the style.

Old overalls were made to fit the smaller children and bits and pieces were used to make mittens. They were lined with the bottoms of Grandma's old flannel nightwear. The cuffs were made out of the ribbing of Dad's old socks which could no longer be mended. The ribbing was extra nice and tight, being made of good quality all-cotton. The wristlets were made long to fit well under the coat sleeves. Long walks to school called for good, warm clothing.

12

1931 Prohibition. Before we piled into my friend's father's Durant car and headed for the dance at Glenwood, we
sneaked down the cellar through the outside door and
grabbed a picnic bottle of home brew.

G.V.
Menomonie, WI

Our cream check for two weeks was 50 cents.

Martha Stevens
Menomonie, WI

My folks had a used furniture store in Eau Claire and they
had to close it up.

Shirley

I tried to dilute the little bit of gas in the car to make
it to town. I added some kerosene. You can't do that.

I can't stand anything, not even a candy bar, with honey
in it. It is all we had for years and years.

Bertice G.
Menomonie, WI

And we never had to leave our home. Taxes were 25 cents
an acre per year. It was always a worry trying to find
the funds to take care of this. And the farm wasn't yours
for long if this was neglected.

H.C.

We lived on the lake. It was my brothers job every day to
go fishing and bring back tubs of blue gills to feed the
pigs. The grain had burned up.

Herb H.

Vitamins was not a word in the dictionary. We knew
instinctively that unless we served a variety of foods our
families would not be well.

H.C.

Women helped the men in the fields and with chores. At noon and in the evenings the women also made the meals and did other household work almost never sitting down. The chickens were womens sole responsibility needing feed three times a day. They put many a good meal on the table.

D.V.

My father was a grocer in Wheeler. He gave groceries away. People had no money to pay.

My father ran the creamery in Connorsville. You bet we knew there were hard times. Cattle were shipped to Sawyer county to survive on leaves.

10 cents worth of gum drops were bought for Christmas. Mother made gum drop fruit cake with them. That and popcorn balls were our entire Christmas treats. A chicken was butchered and Dad made a toy for each.

D.F.

T.B. took all the cows but one.

Over-smoked or salted meat was soaked in milk to make it palatable. Normally water was used.

Del F.

Bacon soaked in milk won't curl in the fry pan.

Del F.

During the Depression, the Popsicle Company offered its two-stick popsicle for 5-cents and suggested the customer split it and share it with a friend.

The Depression was real, but I feel most fortunate to have had a loving Mom who could turn whatever food into something "so good," rejected clothing into something "brand new."

E. Zuerner
East Troy WI

When everything else was dried up our beans still survived. So we had bean soup and baked beans a lot.

D.C. Stensrud

When the gardens were burned up only weeds grew. We ate the weeds.

My husband tells of hard times during the depression and their lunch to take to school was home made bread with lard and sugar or syrup.

My mother used to tell a story, told to her by her father about a man who had a choice of 3 women for a wife and he asked them to cut the rind from cheese. One woman cut too much and was wasteful. One cut to little and the cheese was not good to eat. One just gleaned the very outside layer off, being thirfty and also thorough, so he chose her for his bride.

Enid Drehmel
Eau Claire, WI

Hospital Bill

1933 baby girl (Caloris)

10 days in hospital	$45.00
gas	2.50
drugs	1.25
	$48.75

Meta & Phillip Snow
Menomonie, WI

"My husband was the school principal. His salary was cut. There were four of us at the table. I turned his shirt collars and mended his suits. There wasn't enough to go around, but we were happy".

Meta Snow
Menomonie, WI

"I remember my mother darning my father's and brother's socks with string from the grocery store."

Dorothy Ganong
Eau Claire, WI

"Our neighbor in Forada, MN shipped a car load of sheep. When he got his check he found it didn't pay for the shipping. He owed 37 cents more than the sheep brought".

Lorenz

"A farmer in Starbuck couldn't sell his hogs. No market for them. He also couldn't feed them any longer. So he took them to town and let them loose, for anyone to take who wanted them".

G.V.

Sometimes my daughter thinks I'm "tight", but how can you be any other way when that's the way you were brought up from day 1.

We were fortunate to have apples and plums as Dad had a big orchard and we had a big garden. We also had our own meat and canned with the hot water bath method.

Yes, the drought years of the early thirties, we lived through them of course. Prices were terrible. Banks closed and we lost what we had.

I sold 4 cords of wood for 50 cents.

Shirley Thompson
Menomonie WI

One of my favorite meals was lots of browned fried potatoes with cream poured over. I like it still.

E.C.

"Milk toast, Ugh! Father called it Graveyard stew".

Verna Hein

You can substitute 1/2 egg shell of water for an egg.

At least if you had one dollar you could go and buy groceries.

Mrs. Doug Whinnery
Eau Claire, WI

For Christmas Dad made a wooden wheel barrow for me.

Bannick
Hammond

Oh how I relished my first banana split bought by my
uncle. I thought it would be a banana split in two. We
never had bananas. But when it came, Oh my. I talked
about it for days and remember it still.

Lloyd Bannick
Hammond

We used to pick gooseberries down in the woods for pies
and jelly.

Julie Weiss
Mondovi, WI

I am of the belief that no one knows more about the Great
Depression than I do.

Nothing ever was wasted.

I set up bread from a sponge. I used spook yeast.

Paul Fredrickson NHA
Melrose, WI

Every family knew what it was to live on bread and
Wisconsin Gravy.

Delores Harris
Eau Claire, WI

I grew up during the depression. It was probably a good
education.

Virginia Fyksen
Eau Claire, WI

My mother often made Grot for supper. This was always
true when the home made bread was gone.

I was glad I was brought up in those times as you really learn to appreciate and take care of things.

Alma Smith
Woodville, WI

I was born in 1931 and I didn't know it was bad. Grown ups didn't tell us their troubles.

We had some sows and they'd have little ones so when they grew big enough we'd butcher one.

When we butchered my Dad used to say we used all but the squeal.

We didn't have beef very often at all. Unless the cow didn't get pregnant or broke a leg or something.

We had a lot of bread pudding. We had bread, eggs and milk.

Audrey Samplowski
Chetek, WI

We had plain bread with milk poured over for supper.

And we had toasted bread with blackberries thickened with cornstarch over it for breakfast.

"Yes! They were heartbreaking years to remember".

Linda M. Weber
Chippewa Falls, WI

Ed and Barbara Klimek of Millerville, MN, were married in 1935. The Four R's, a five-piece band, played for their wedding dance at a cost of $7.00, but the band members gave the bride and groom $1.00 as a wedding gift.

Ed and Barbara's first crop failed because of the drought.

Few people were buying diamond rings, but Howard Olson was young and for his bride to be the very best was hardly good enough. The jeweler went along with $1.00 a week payment. However, Howard didn't earn much more than that, and whenever he went to visit his sweetheart, the payment was sometimes held up. Gasoline was 19-cents a gallon.

"Gardening was the main source of ones living. The whole family worked in it too".

Alma Smith
Woodville, WI

"The chief priority on the farm was to feed the animals and ourselves".

Betty Ewer
Holcombe, WI

Grandmother's Sandwich Spread

1 c. molasses, 1/2 c. butter, and 3 eggs beaten. Add butter to molasses and heat to boiling point. Add eggs and cook 'til thick. This is an old recipe from

Mrs. Ted B.
Lebanon, TN

I recently read about a manager of one of the White Front drugstores in Seattle. Seems that during the depression he made sandwiches selling for 5 cents which had the following filling:- 1 qt. bread crumbs, 1 sm. can tuna, 1 c. cod liver oil. This mixture was sufficient for 50 sandwiches. He claims he couldn't keep up with the demand.

E. Stacy
Selah, WA

"Those were the Good Old Days".

Enid Drehmel
Fall Creek, WI

Mrs. Clarence Walters recalls her family toasting and grinding barley to replace coffee. They learned to enjoy the rich toasted flavor of the grain.

Menomonie, WI

Introduction

The good food served in the 30's, in spite of the hard times and the burned our gardens, provided nutritious meals, though there never was quite enough to go around. Our large senior citizen population attests to the quality of the food. Children of that era today are getting older and many are still enjoying good health, while some mothers who cooked those meals are still here to tell us their stories.

The recipes in this book are primarily from the 1930's or when food preservatives were unknown. Recipes used were gleaned from grandmother's files, not from old cookbooks, as remembered and told to the children of the mothers who cooked these meals.

BIG BREAKFASTS

For Hungry Families

Breakfast for Hearty Appetites

The first meal of the day was by necessity a big meal. Everyone was hungry and it would be a long time before dinner or lunch if you went to school. Furthermore, country people had already put in several hours of demanding physical work and a large breakfast was in order.

Anna Clech of Menomonie, WI., prepared a large pan of oatmeal so there would surely be lots of left overs for supper. Any cereal left over from breakfast was packed into loaf pans and chilled in the pantry. In the evening it was sliced and fried in lard till brown on both sides and served with corn syrup out of a half gallon pail. Anna's children even today remember that they never tired of this delicious fried oatmeal supper.

The oatmeal used was the old fashioned long cooking variety. Quick cooking oats does not lend itself to many of these good dishes and is not as flaky for breakfast cereal.

Oatmeal was served with milk or cream which ever was available and with honey or sugar if it could be spared.

Helen Cichy of Minnesota lent variety to her breakfasts with serving wheat berries directly from the granary. Wheat was washed and using a heavy pan was covered with water, covered with a good lid and brought to a boil. Proportions are 1 c. of wheat berries to 2 c. of water. Once boiling it was moved back on the wood stove to simmer for several hours. It was warmed up in the morning and was served with rich milk or light cream and honey. Brown sugar was also used when it was available.

To provide vitamin C when there were no oranges available the German settlements relied heavily on sauerkraut for dinner. Tomatoes were used at breakfast served in a berry bowl with sugar added and cream poured over all. It was exceptionally good with fresh bread and coffee.

Morning coffee was always full strength with the children sometimes having a half cup with whole milk added to fill the cup. Throughout the day water was added to the grounds and brought to a boil for further refreshment, or at least something to drink with a lunch or meal.

Cornmeal and Mush

Everyone "tried" to keep buckwheat flour for pancakes and cornmeal for mush on hand. With these two items in the house you were still eating.

However, some pantries were not always so well stocked. Paul Fredrickson of Elmwood, Wisconsin remembers May 18, 1933. They woke up with one egg and one cup of flour in the house and no money.

Almost everyone used cornmeal as one of the staple foods during the hard times. Some relied on it more and became experts at preparations, and variations.

Such was the the case in the Cecil B. family when he was a young man. He still enjoys it so much today he bakes it himself to make sure it is prepared just right.

Cecil says the buttermilk recipes are by far the best and the following is one of them.

Buttermilk Johnny Cake

Sift together:

| 1 c. | flour, sifted | 3/4 t. | baking soda |
| 1 t. | salt | 1 t. | baking powder |

Mix with 1 c. cornmeal.

Combine:
1/4 c. shortening, melted   2   eggs, well beaten

Add to:
1-1/2 c. buttermilk (sour milk can be used too)

Combine with flour mixture and beat only till smooth. Fill well greased shallow pan. Bake at 425F for 25 min.

Serve with syrup and fried pork or sausages. Cecil recalls the children eating it with milk and sugar for their supper. Others used milk only. It was one of the basic foods that was served often for supper. Cecil Brehn

2 T. of brown sugar can be added to the above recipe for those who enjoy their Johnny Cake sweet. The real die hard Johnny Cake eaters rarely used a sweetener in their recipes.

Popular Johnny Cake

Another favorite recipe using no white flour is the following:-

Melt: 2 T.   fat

Add: 2   eggs, well beaten
           1 t.   salt

Add: 2 c.   sour milk

And:-   2 c.   cornmeal with] Mix only
           1 t.   soda   ] to moisten.

Bake at 400F for 20 to 25 min.
Instead of using shortening in the corn bread batter
cracklings were sometimes used. Cracklings were the crisp
brown bits left from frying out the lard on hog butchering
days.

                                    Doris Cronk
                                    Menomonie, WI.

Cornbread using Sugar

1	egg	2 t.	baking powder
3 T.	sugar	1/2 t.	soda
1 c.	sour milk	1/2 t.	salt
4 T.	lard	1 c.	cornmeal
1 c.	flour		

Bake at 425F for 25 min. Favorite recipe in many homes.

                                    Norma Niceswanger
                                    Chetek, WI.

Mrs. S. Waite believes the leanest breakfast of those
days was a water pudding made out of flour and water
cooked to porridge consistency. Anything that filled the
stomach was better than nothing.

Cornmeal Mush

This often-used dish was prepared for breakfast and the left overs, packed in bread tins and cooled in the pantry were sliced and fried for supper, or the evening meal. It was dipped in flour and fried crisp and delicious in fat. It was generally served with syrup which was plentiful.

To cook mush with no lumps:-
Mix:- 1 c. cornmeal with 4 c. water. Bring to a boil, add 1 t. salt and cook gently for a t least 30 min. to get the best flavor out of the cornmeal. Serve with top milk (half and half) and sugar. Or mix 1 c. cornmeal with 1 c. water. Add to 3 c. boiling water with salt added, stirring continuously.

Carnation Pancakes

Beat:-   6   eggs, slightly

Add:-   dash   salt
           1 can   Carnation milk (12 oz.)

Mix and Add:-
           1/2 c. flour Or enough for a very thin batter.

Pour from pitcher into hot fat, baking one at a time. Turn and lift pan to make dinner plate size pancake. Serve with syrup and sausages.

Janet's Buttermilk Pancakes

1 c.	buttermilk	2	eggs
1/2 t.	salt	1 T.	sugar
1 T.	shortening, melted	1 t.	soda
some	flour to thicken		

Mix and fry on greased griddle.

My parents had a large family and not much else, but they managed to be happy. That warmth still extends to the entire family today. Mom made good food out of practically nothing.

G. Frey
Menomonie Falls WI.

Buttermilk Pancakes from Martha

This is a light pancake that no one ever tires of. It is
as popular today as it was then, and it is nourishing.

Sift together:-
```
1 c.      flour
1-1/2 t.  baking powder
1/2 t.    soda
1 T.      sugar
1/2 t.    salt
```

Add:
```
1 c.      buttermilk
1         egg, beaten
1 T.      oil
```

Bake on hot griddle. Serves 2 to 4.

Martha Stevens
Menomonie, WI.

Squash Griddle Cakes

```
2 c.      squash, cooked and mashed
some      salt
1 T.      sugar
2 c.      milk
1         egg
1 c       flour, sifted
```

Mix all together and fry on hot griddle. Good for
breakfast or lunch.

Sourdough Pancakes

Using glass or pottery bowl; Mix:-
```
1         cake yeast
2 c.      flour
2 c.      warm water
```

Beat well. Let stand in warm place or closed cupboard
overnight or 8 hrs.

```
Add:-   2        eggs   ] Beat well.
        1 t.     salt   ] Add 2 T. melted fat.
        1 T.     sugar  ] Bake on hot griddle.
```

27

Beef Patty Breakfast

Mix:-   1 lb.   hamburger, lean, and fry till gray.
Drain.

Add: 1 clove   garlic
        1/2   onion, grated
        some   salt and pepper (savory salt is good)

Mix with:-   4   coarsely grated peeled potatoes cooked, but preferably with jackets on. Form patties and fry.

This was a wood cutting breakfast. Today we call it Hunters Breakfast.

Oatmeal and Apple

Blend:-   1 c.   oatmeal
         2 c.   water
         1/2 t.   salt

Bring to boil; cover pan and let simmer 10 min. Add 2 grated apples and 1/2 t. cinnamon. Cover and cook till apples are done. Serve with honey and milk.

Breakfast Apples

Use for French toast, Pancakes, Waffles or as a sauce for most anything.

1/3 c.   brown sugar   ] Mix
1/2 c.   flour   ] well.

Add:-   1/3 c.   water and stir

Add 2 sliced apples and cook till apples are done. Serve hot.

Glenda W.
St. Paul, MN.

Xtra Light Beer Biscuits

No other biscuits quite compare to these feather light creations.

2 c.	flour, sifted
3 t.	baking powder
1/2 t.	salt
4 T.	cold shortening, cut into the above.
3 T.	sugar
1 can	beer, can be warm and stale.

Drop in muffin tins or roll out, knead and cut. Bake at 375F till browned.

The First Waffle

"My grandchildren love the story of the first waffle". It is said to have been made in the 13th Century England. A crusader wearing his armor accidently sat in some freshly baked oat cakes. The cakes were flattened and bore deep imprints of the steel links. However, he spread butter on the cakes and ate them. His wife, delighted with the way the butter stayed in the imprints from the armor, made him put it on once a week and sit on fresh oat cakes. They were called "Warfres", meaning flat honeycomb cakes. Dutch colonists brought their cherished "Warfres" irons to America. They were long handled and very heavy to hold over an open fire".

Enid Drehmel
Fall Creek, WI

Bill Garnett of Menomonie, Wisconsin, says he didn't have it so bad through the Great Depression. His family had a variety. They either had oatmeal, farina or cornmeal mush for their meals.

But Sundays were a different story, Bill remembers. His mother would add a handful of raisins to the oatmeal and with her expertise, they became deliciously light, fluffy and juicy. Sunday was a day to look forward to.

Herding Cattle

Lyle Stratton of Menomonie, Wisconsin, was a young ma
helping his father operate the family farm in the 1930's
They had 12 cows to feed and 5 children to support. Whe
the drought hit the area and the pastures burned away
Lyle's father went north looking for green pasture. He wa
lucky. At Minong he found 40 acres with a spring on it fo
$1.00 an acre. He lost no time purchasing it, but th
cream checks came a long way from paying for the land.

Lyle was elected to herd the cattle that summer. He buil
the fence by fastening barbed wire to the trees. A three
sided tarpaulin nailed to trees provided living shelte
Lyle says he was comfortable enough. There was no rain
so he needed little protection from that, and the sprin
not only watered the cattle, but also cooled the milk.

One wonders about his eating habits since the cream check
were low ($2.00 at most, and once it was a mere 7-cents.
He framed this one to remember the day he felt it reall
couldn't get much worse.

**Meals in a dish, Casseroles,
and Cooking from the Garden**

We lived by the river, which was our salvation. We not only were able to raise a garden when everyone else's was drying up, but we also had a good potato crop. In winter when hay for the cattle was gone, we boiled potatoes for the animals to keep them going until spring.

I remember having one set of underwear which I washed every night. Our school bus was a horse-drawn sleigh with a little house built on it. It was cozy with a stove in the center, even though it cooled off each time the door opened for another family of children to enter.

The men kept the roads open by plowing with a drag piled heavy with rocks. It kept a lot of the neighbors busy in the winter getting us to and from school.

Anita Nevin
Menomonie WI

The Garfield Halverson's were fortunate in 1931. They were married that year and they both had work. They were paid $15.00 a month for both of them working grueling long days on a farm. They had to provide their own board out of their earnings, and they did their best to find spare time in which to raise a vegetable garden. Mrs. Halverson remembers some very nice tomatoes she raised that year which she planned to coldpack for winter use. But they were due for a shock when they woke up on August 23, 1931 to a heavy frost on the ground. Needless to say, all the tomatoes were frozen. Mrs. Halverson was so heartbroken she just can't forget that fateful day so long ago.

If you ladle two tablespoons of milk over sliced beef liver and let it stand for 10 minutes, it will take any strong taste away.

J. Keen
Bloomingdale IL

R.H. Brunswick of Augusta WI earned 26-1/2 cents an hour doing construction work. His job was swinging a 16-pound sledge all day long. When he found a truckdriving job with George Massey of Menomonie, he didn't hesitate to take it. However, he had to stay at the hotel for this job and the bedbugs almost drove him out.

Meals in a dish, Casseroles, and Cooking from the Garden

I was born in 1920, so the Great Depression is a
very vivid part of my life. I had two brothers
younger than me. When I was three my father was
taken to a Veteran's Hospital. He never
recovered and died when I was six years old. My
mother moved to live with her parents on a small
farm.

We were more fortunate to live on a farm than in
a town or city. The chief priority on the farm
was to feed the animals and ourselves.

During the drought we hauled water for the
gardens. My mother and grandmother canned everything they could get their hands on for food.

I remember once my grandfather took a case of
eggs to the grocer's. He wanted 10 cents a dozen
and the grocer offered him 8 cents a dozen. He
brought them home and dumped them in the pig
trough.

I remember a letter to be mailed might sit on the
buffet for two or three weeks before there was 2
cents to buy a stamp to mail it.

As tough as it was there was peace and happiness
and a family love and respect that is nearly gone
these days. We learned how to work.

Betty Ewers
Holcombe, WI

When we hear that women made meals out of practically nothing we can believe it. The following is a recipe used very often by the mother of Frank Seitz of Altoona, WI. Similar to shpatzen or spaetsle, it is a solid dumpling served in a variety of ways. Women invented their own favorites and this one is remembered as a good meal "mother used to make".

Glaze

"Glaze? Yes! You take enough flour for the amount of dough you want, 2 eggs, and salt to taste. Milk to thin the dough a little so you can spoon it into a kettle of hot boiling water. Spoon so you have the size of our chicken nuggets of today. Cook till done.

Drain off water and put into a serving dish. In the meantime have prepared 2 med. sized onions sliced and fried in bacon grease. Then while still very hot pour over the glaze for a very tasty and fulfilling meal".

Frank Seitz
Altoona, WI

"Handed down through a genealogy record the gravy dates back to 1856 THE YEAR OF WISCONSIN GRAVY. How do you make gravy without meat or butter or milk"?

"Well, put the spider on the stove, then put some watter in the spider, then put some flour in a cup, put some watter over it and mix it up together, when the watter boils, stur in the mixture, put some salt and pepper in to season it."

From the records of: Mrs. Dolores Harris
                                         Eau Claire, WI

Another meal enjoyed in Michigan is remembered by Anne Meulemans of Downing, WI. It is potatoes cooked and served as is on a dinner plate. Thick, cool clabbered milk was served in bowls into which the potatoes were dipped before eating.

Today we use sour cream on our baked potatoes but no doubt are no tastier than were the potatoes and clabbered milk of those days gone by.

Wild Rice Venison Casserole

Sounds like a luxury dish today. Wild rice was cheap in the 30's and because of harvest locale it survived the drought longer than the area gardens did.

Dredge in flour 1 lb. venison

Brown in:
3 T.   bacon fat   1/2   onion

Add all in 3 qt. baking pan:-
1 clove   garlic, minced
2 c.   canned tomatoes
1/2 c.   green pepper, diced (optional)
1-1/2 t. salt, pepper (seasoned salt is good)
1/4 t.   curry powder
1/2 t.   chili powder

Parboil:-
1 c.   raw washed wild rice
1-1/2 c. water

Boil rice till almost tender. Add to above and bake at 350F for 1 hr.

* * *

"Macaroni and Tomatoes and Tomatoes and Macaroni, all the time. I still like it today with variations".

Ellen

Baked Macaroni and Tomatoes

Add:-
2 T.   fat, melted (bacon fat is good)
1/2 t.   salt
1 can   tomatoes (1 qt.)

Arrange in layers with:-
2 c.   cooked macaroni

Cover generously with buttered crumbs. Bake in hot oven till heated through and crumbs are brown.

35

Scalloped Tomatoes

Fill a well oiled baking dish with:-
2 c.   tomatoes, alternating with —
1 c.   bread cubes, season between layers and —
dot   with butter.

Cover with crumbs and bake for 35 min. or until nicely browned.

When gardens grew everyone had home canned tomatoes. These side dishes were a tasty addition to any table.

Pigs In Potato Patch

Another depression dish which "looked like a lot" was this huge appetizing bowl of mashed potatoes with cooked wieners, cut in half, and stuck into the potatoes all over. Milk or cream gravy accompanied this satifying meal. Weiners were 3 cents a pound and were all meat. No sweepings.

A similar meal served many many times in Wheeler Wisconsin called for half a ring of bologna cut up into tiny pieces which were added to the milk gravy. The other half of the bologna was saved for the next day. The clever cook who served this could afford bologna because they owned the grocery store. Country people only had it for a rare Sunday Dinner.

Further use of a portion of a ring of bologna was made by resourceful cooks in adding it to scalloped, fried, or creamed potatoes. In Hammond, Wisconsin half the ring of bologna was used for dinner at noon. In the evening they had the other half, ground with stretchings, eggs, cereal, and whatever lent itself to sandwich spread for supper.

Dum Dum Depression Casserole

As copied from the Doc Severinson Tonight Show by the mother of Virginia Fyksen, Eau Claire, Wisconsin.

In a buttered casserole arrange sliced potatoes and onion rounds. Fry pork sausage and pour off grease. Alternate with a can of whole kernel corn and seasoning. Pour a can of tomato soup on top. (Canned tomatoes were probably used also) Bake till done, depending on size of casserole.

Grit Wurst

From the German community comes this everlasting favorite. The recipe calls for a hogs head which one can buy today at butcher shops, or anywhere where butchering is done. The cost is small when considering the many good meals it provides.

Boil one hog's head in water to cover until meat falls off bones. This takes a canner as a cooking vessel. Remove to large platter to cool. Remove fat parts and use lean only. Grind meat and add a lot of allspice, salt and pepper to taste. Add equal parts of cooked oatmeal. Pack in bread tins and freeze or store in refrigerator. Slice and fry for lunches or a nourishing breakfast.

The Bohemian version calls for barley cooked and used in place of the oatmeal. Dry bread was added and salt, pepper and garlic flavored this dish. Still others like the cornmeal mush base. All these dishes were staples in the 1930's because they stretched the meat and were satisfying.

> Dorothy Van Amber
> Alexandria MN

I'm sure my kids thought I was kidding when I told them about some of the "meal stretchers."

> P. Malmer
> Milwaukee WI

Cornmeal Mush and Pork

To make a more filling meal out of the fried cornmeal mush and to vary the menu since it was served so often, the following recipe was used.

Simmer 1 lb. pork with bones or any meat and bones left over until very tender. Remove meat and bones and boil broth down to 1 qt. (or add water). Add 1 t. salt and 1/2 t. sage. Add 1 c. cornmeal dissolved in 1 c. of cold water. Add to broth and cook until it thickens, stirring frequently. Add shredded meat. Pour into greased bread loaf pans; chill; slice, dip in flour and fry in fat till brown and crispy. Serve hot with syrup or apple breakfast topping.

Head Cheese

Cook until meat falls off bones in salted water, one hog's head and one hog's tongue. Shred and season with salt and pepper, or with chili powder. Pack tightly in a bowl, cover and weight it down. Let stand 3 days in a cold place. Slice and serve.

My father liked bread and milk and head cheese for Sunday supper. Head cheese was made from cooking the bones and any meat from the freshly butchered pig's head. Sage, salt and pepper were the seasonings used.

Doris Cronk
Menomonie, WI.

Rabbits and Squirrels

There were many cotton tail rabbits on our farm. They were dressed and frozen and were ready when needed. Mother dipped the cut up pieces in flour and fried them in bacon fat until golden brown. She made cream gravy with pan drippings and always served it with Johnny Cake (cornbread).

Doris Cronk

I shot squirrels on Hank Daniel's Island by the dozen.

G.V.

38

Hominy

Each fall we children chose the choicest ear corn from the crib and helped shell it. The kernels were boiled in lye water in the big copper boiler on the kitchen wood range. When the hard outer shell of each kernel loosened, the white inside kernels were washed many times. Salt was added. They were packed in sterile jars and cold pack processed. Pork chops, hominy and rich pork chop cream gravy made a tummy filling meal.

Doris Cronk
Menomonie, WI.

Howard Helgeson of Ridgeland, Wisconsin, remembers his family relying heavily on wild game for food in the 1930's. He became very adept at preparing gourmet wildlife dinners. Several of his choicest follow:

Hunter's Partridge

Using 4 dressed and washed partridges, sprinkle inside and out with salt and pepper. Mix 4 cups shredded cabbage and 4 slices fried and crumbled bacon. Spoon 1/4 mixture into each bird. Wrap each with 4 cabbage leaves and tie with string. Place in large skillet. Mix 3 T. butter, 1 c. chicken stock or bouillon cube, 4 slices carrots, 1/4 t. each of thyme, tarragon and pepper and 1 t. salt. Pour over partridges. Bring to boil; reduce heat, cover and simmer 30 min., or until done. Serve with pan sauce.

Creamed, Fried Partridges

Using 2 birds, cut into serving pieces and dredge with seasoned flour. Fry salt pork until crisp. Remove from par and fry partridges in fat. When brown, add crisp pork. Pour 1 c. thick cream or evaporated milk over all. Cover and simmer until done.

Wild Greens

Children gathered springtime dandelions and cowslip greens to be cooked and served with vinegar.

Doris C.

Dandelion Dinner

No meal was more eagerly awaited for and enjoyed with more relish than the springtime dandelion dinner. The best dandelions were found partially under leaves. They were gathered by the dishpan full as soon as they made their appearance. To clean them the top of the leaves were held together while the bottom root part was cut away. After shaking out the very inner growth and discarding it, the tender stems and leaves were put into another large pan and were thoroughly washed.

Bacon or side pork was fried and removed to a serving dish. Vinegar was added to an equal part of drippings in the pan. Several hard boiled eggs were sliced over the cut up greens, a potato was crushed into it, hot from the boiled potato kettle, and the vinegar dressing was poured over hot from the stove. The large salad was tossed lightly and served with the boiled potatoes and side pork or bacon. No gravy was needed or ever wanted with this dinner. The unique piquant flavor of the greens blended just right with the plain mealy potatoes. Very large bowls of this salad were consumed as long as the dandelions were in season. Today we use fresh endive.

Dandelions were also prepared by steaming them and adding a similar dressing. They were popular in most communities as were another green called lambs quarters. These were always steamed and prepared like spinach. By the time the dandelion season came to an end the young beets were sprouting their tender leaves, except through the drought, when only weeds grew. These greens survived the dry weather longer than the gardens and grains did. They were used as long as they could be found.

The drought was a climatic disaster lasting from 1933 to 1937.

"My 6 yr. old brother Omar had never experienced rain. When it finally did come pouring down he ran to the house and excitedly cried that "the lake was falling down".

D.C. Stensrud

Cottage Cheese or Dutch Cheese

Mother made cottage cheese by placing a large pan of clabbered sour milk at the side back of the wood range where it would heat slowly. When the milk separated, she strained it through a cloth. The whey was fed to the pigs. Nothing was wasted. Salt and fresh cream were added to the cheese curds and it was ready to use.

Doris Cronk

A typical supper was fresh cottage cheese, raw fried potatoes, bread and butter pickles and bread. It was a very good meal.

From Mondovi:- "I don't think it can be made from processed milk. Sometimes Dutch Cheese and vegetables from the garden was all we had to eat along with home made bread or my 4 dozen baking powder biscuits I made every week. It was good. Mom made 9 loaves of bread twice a week and I made biscuits in-between".

We were a family of 12 children so we all had to help. It seemed that every itinerant salesman, horse trader or tramp arrived at our house at meal time. My Dad's philosophy was "there is always room for one more".

Julie Weiss
Mondovi, WI.

Weeks before berry picking time, even blossoms were used as a means of adding variety to meals. Elderberries were plentiful in Wisconsin, and Lu Grothe of Durand recalls picking the blossoms and enjoying the crisp fried treats it provided.

The blossoms with stems left on were dipped in beaten egg and dipped in flour before frying to a golden crunchy brown in the big old fry pan using lard. Sometimes a flour egg batter was used. You took them by the stem to eat them and they were marvelous, the Durand ladies remember. Similar egg and flour quick-fix meals follow.

Cottage Cheese Dressing

Beat together:-

1/2 c.	milk		1/4 c.	honey or sugar
1/2 t.	salt		1/2 c.	vinegar
3/4 t.	dry mustard		1/2 t.	paprika
1/2 c.	cottage cheese			

Dressing may reach desired thickening by chilling. Dab of whipped cream on top of individual plates may top salad.

Elly Kelly
Eau Claire, WI

Schmorn (also, Schmarren) or Kratser

"One recipe my Mom made quite often was Schmorn (Schmarren). It can be made from any number of eggs, a little more milk than you'd use for scrambled eggs, a little sugar, salt and baking powder and enough flour to make a thin batter, like a very thin pancake batter. She fried it in butter in a hot black iron skillet, stirring and turning it until it was a golden brown. Delicious!

My husband's mother made it by adding bread crumbs to the egg-milk mixture, with a pinch of salt, sugar and no baking powder, until all liquid is absorbed. I still make it for him occasionally."

Julie Weiss

Kratser

This is a similar dish, also economical and very tasty and satisfying. These dishes were made many times a week and the families never tired of them.

Fry bacon cut into small pieces. Pour over it a batter made of 3 eggs, 1/2 c. milk and 1/2 c. flour and seasoning. Stir and turn until it is a golden brown like omelets. Pork cracklings were also used in this dish.

42

Another Kratzen and Schmorn this is:

Lazy Pancakes

5 eggs, salt, milk, and flour made this simple easy dish.
Bacon drippings were heated in the large heavy skillet,
the above was mixed well and it was poured into the hot
grease. With a pancake turner it was turned over and over
until all was cooked, light, fluffy and brown.

It was served with one of the sauces made from berries or
rhubarb, cornstarch and sugar, or with syrup from the
gallon pail.

H. Cichy

Lazy Pancakes (or Schmorn/Schmarren, or Kratzen) kept many
a family from going to bed hungry.

This version of the Schmorn/Schmarren comes from the
mother of a Whitehall lady:

"My mother heated 2 c. of milk, broke up dry bread, as
much as could be absorbed and poured three or four beaten
eggs with salt and pepper and a pinch of sugar and fried
it in a pan. Good!"

Garden Casserole

This meal was made by the roaster full and there was
seldom any left. A reduced recipe follows:

Grease a casserole very well.
Slice 2   onions into it
Add: 4   potatoes, sliced thin
2 c.   corn, canned or fresh
1 lb.   pork sausage, fried and drained
1 t.   salt
1/4 t.   pepper

2 c. canned or fresh tomatoes poured over all. Buttered
crumbs as topping. Bake with cover on 30 min., finish
baking till done and a crusty brown.

Layered Garden Casserole

In a large casserole arrange a layer of each. Season between each layer (lightly).

```
1 layer    potatoes
1 layer    onion rings
1 layer    dry rice (3/4 c.)
1 layer    peas
1 lb.      hamburger, fried and drained
1 qt.      tomatoes (or 1 can)
3 slices   bacon
```

Bake for 2 hrs. in slow oven or until done. Cover 1st, half hour.

So Good Casserole

```
1 lb.      ground beef, browned with:
1/3 c.     onions, chopped
Add:
1 qt.      tomatoes (or 1 can)
2 t.       salt
Cook:
1-1/2 c. spaghetti
```

Alternate in casserole dish with 1 c. corn and beef tomato mixture. Bake at 350F for 1 hr.

Potato Casserole

Sauté 1/4 c. butter with 1 med. chopped onion

Add: 2-1/2 T. flour in fry pan

Add gradually: 2 c.   milk
                  some   salt and pepper

In greased casserole dish alternate above with 3 c. cubed cooked potatoes and 1/2 c. shredded mild cheese. Shred some cheese on top. Bake at 350F for 25 to 35 min.

Fish Casserole

Any filleted fish can be used for this. Fresh water pan
fish filleted are very nice for this dish.

Butter casserole dish well. Arrange fish in it and cover
lightly with cream (half & half). Cover with fine bread
crumbs. Bake till fish flakes and crust is brown and
bubbly. Serve with cooked fresh peas arranged around
dish.

Del

Boiled Ham Dinner

Simmer a picnic or ham hock with a lot of ham left on it.
Add no salt.

Add:
6 sm.	carrots
6	turnips, cut in quarters
6 sm.	onions
6	potatoes, peeled

Cook till vegetables are done. Meanwhile steam one small
head of cabbage cut in 1/8ths. With slotted spoon arrange
vegetables in center of serving platter. Arrange cabbage
around edge. Place ham overall. Drizzle butter over
cabbage and vegetables.

Country Ham & Potato Supper

Alternate:
8 sliced	potatoes
1/2 lb.	ham, cut up
2 T.	flour
1 t.	salt
1/8 t.	pepper
2 T.	onion, grated
2 T.	butter

Pour scalded milk to almost cover. Bake in covered dish
for 30 min. Uncover and bake till brown and done.

45

English Monkey

Soak: 1 c.   bread crumbs in;
           1 c.   milk

Melt: 1 T.   fat

Add: 1/2 c. mild cheese, grated

Add to crumb mixture. Beat 1 egg add to the above with salt and pepper; cook 3 min. Pour over toast and serve.

Bavarion Potato Dodge

Grate or grind 3 lbs. raw potatoes*

Add: 1 c.   flour
         1   egg
         some salt and pepper

Mix well and pour into well greased 8x12" pan. Potatoes must be drained in colander before adding ingredients. Bake for 30 min. at 350F. Add lean side pork strips and bake till pork is crisp and potatoes are done. Cut in squares and serve.

This was often enjoyed on cold winter days as a supper dish. * The starch from the drained potatoes was washed, dried and used for cooking.

Margaret Cichy

Door County Fish Boil

A favorite now, it was also a popular low cost dish in the 1930's. It wasn't always served with a lot of melted butter as we know it today, but it was served nevertheless because of it's economy and availability of fish in some areas. Served in proportions for family or neighborhood gatherings, a large cooking vessel was needed.

Cook 15 lbs. of peeled potatoes whole for 12 min. in a lot of water. Add 10 peeled onions and cook 5 min. more. Add 10 lbs. fish fillets and 5 c. salt and cook 8 min. more. With slotted spoon serve directly on plates, drizzle with melted butter.

Corn Pudding

Scalloped corn, puddings, Indian corn, whatever they called it, everyone made it, a lot.

Mix: 1 pt.   corn
             2   eggs, beaten

Add: 1 t.   salt
             1/8 t.   pepper
             2 T.   melted bacon drippings
             2 T.   sugar

Pour into greased baking dish and bake until knife comes out clean. Bake in 350F oven.

Scalloped Corn

Combine: 3 c.   corn
         2   eggs, beaten
         1/2 t. salt

Using 3/4 c. crumbs, alternate layers with corn mixture. Dot with butter. Add: 1 c. milk. Bake at 325F for about 30 min.

Betty's Potato Pancakes

Grind or grate 3 large potatoes and drain off water using a colander.

Add:
3   eggs
1 t.   soda
1 t.   baking powder
1 t.   salt

Add:
1-1/2 c. flour or enough for a thin batter mixed with 1-1/2 c. milk. Fry in greased griddle to crusty brown.

Betty F.
Turtle Lake, WI.

Old Time Baked Beans

No meal planning was complete without a good recipe for baked beans. Recipes varied but they all were good and very nourishing. Men needed something to stay with them in their physical work and it did replace meat when that was not in plentiful supply.

Cook beans by adding cold water to 2 c. washed beans to stand an inch above the beans. Put on simmer and bring to a boil slowly. This will take several hours but will be worth it. Beans will be whole and tender. Do not ever add soda for quick cooking. It destroys the vitamins and will result in mushy beans.

Put in a large bean cooker or roaster:

the	precooked beans
1/4 lb.	salt pork or bacon or ham hock
2-1/2 c.	water
1 t.	salt (except when using ham)
1 t.	dry mustard
2 T.	molasses or more
2 T.	brown sugar
1 T.	vinegar
1/2	onion, grated

Salt pork or bacon should be browned and grease poured off. Combine everything. Bake in hot oven at 450F for 15 min. covered. Uncover and bake at least 45 min. longer or until brown but not dry. Water can be added to keep the dish moist.

On a Sunday in Downing WI., Anne M.'s mother would provide a very special treat for the family by adding 2 or 3 cooked prunes per person to the beans, Anne recalls.

With no refrigeration available in the 1930's, it was necessary to preserve the hams and deliciously cured bacon by burying them in the granary oatbin. When seeding time came and the oatbins became lean and bare, Howard Helgeson of Ridgeland, Wisconsin, remembers his mother cold-packing the ham for summer use. She also cold-packed fresh hams, which made meal preparations simple in the busy summer season. The meat and gravy was all prepared in the jars and it didn't take long to get the rest of the meal on.

Hamburger Stretch

1 lb.	hamburger
2 c.	oatmeal
some	onion, grated
1	egg

Mix and season to taste. This was a popular dish when meat was rationed through the war.

Alma Smith
Woodville, WI.

Shkubanky

Is a simple meal in itself. It is Czeck in origin but similar forms of Potato Cakes were also favorites of other areas. These called for:- mashed potatoes, flour and enough potato water to make a stiff dough. Lard was heated in the big fry pan and these cakes were dipped in flour, egg and bread crumbs and fried a crispy brown on both sides. Ground poppy seed or grated cottage cheese was served with this meal.

Marie Larson
Rice Lake, WI

Homemade Noodles

Combine:

1	egg, beaten
1/2 t.	salt
2 T.	milk
1 c.	flour or enough to make stiff dough.

Roll very thin on floured board; let stand 20 min. Roll up loosely; cut into strips. Spread out to dry 2 hrs. Cook or freeze. To dry freshly made noodles hang over the back of a towel covered chair.

(More Depression Noodle recipes on page 53.)

Cod Fish Gravy

Everyone looked forward to Friday when Cod fish gravy was coming up. Salt cod fish was purchased and this had to be cut into small pieces. Soak cod fish in water for three hrs. changing water every hr. to remove the salt. (Today's cod fish may not need this)

Heat 1-1/2 c. milk in double boiler; add drained cod fish. Cook for 10 min. and blend in:

2 T.	butter with
2 T.	flour
1/8 t.	pepper (no salt)

Stir into milk and cod fish. Cook another 10 min. Serve on potatoes mashed or plain boiled.

Mary F. Van Amber
Alexandria, MN

See Gravy for biscuits and potatoes under Bread section.

Joyce's Thistledown Dumplings

Her slight of hand is easily duplicated to produce these tender puffs.

Batter is dropped on chicken or meat in pan, not in broth. It is cooked uncovered for 10 min. She uses a domed cover to prevent soggy dumplings.

Sift:	1-1/2 c.	flour, sifted
	2 t.	baking powder
	3/4 t.	salt

Cut in:	3 T.	Crisco or shortening
Add:	3/4 c.	milk only till blended

Cook gently 10 min. uncovered and 10 min covered. Serve at once, arranging dumplings around platter and meat in center. Make gravy; pour some over all and serve the rest to pass.

Joyce Stanley
Minnetonka, MN

Potato Dumplings

Not to be outdone by other ethnic dishes, the potato dumpling can hold it's own. Equally popular with the German and Norwegian people this is a carry over from the immigrants. It is loved almost as much today by people that have become familiar with it as it was then. However, the long preparation does not adapt to our life style now and is generally served only at ethnic church suppers. Even there, it is becoming hard to find women who remember the very touch it takes to duplicate the exquisite finished product.

The potato dumpling in it's variations was very popular through the Great Depression because of it's available ingredients. Again, the combination of flour and potatoes and bread, assembled in a unique method to arrive at such a delicious popular dish, is nothing short of genuine art.

Lefsa belongs in the same category requiring a skill not everyone can emulate.

Crusty brown potato pancakes were everyone's favorite. They were served regularly because they provided a delicious, inexpensive meal everyone looked forward to. Served with syrup or applesauce, little else was needed at this meal. Another good recipe follows:

Tasty Potato Pancakes

Grate six med. potatoes and 1 small onion. Drain. Add 1 slightly beaten egg and 1/2 c. milk. Stir into potatoes. Add 1 c. flour and 1 t. salt. Cook on griddle till crisp and brown.

Betty Ewer
Holcombe, WI

German Raw Potato Dumplings

Grind raw potatoes to make 2 c. Put in a colander to drain. Press out some of the liquid and keep covered with plastic to keep it from turning dark.

Add: 1 c.   heel of bread cubes
           3/4 t.   salt
           1   egg

Mix very well. Add 1 c. flour or less mixing in very well and form into golf ball size. Roll in flour before adding to ham broth. A bit of cooked ham inside the dumpling is worth the effort.

A ham bone with lots of meat left on makes a good base for this dish. Chicken is also used in some kitchens and should be a stewing chicken, browned, and cooked gently for several hrs. with water to cover. Success of the potato dumpling is in using as little flour as possible and still have the mixture hold together. The finished product should be rather light although most often it will be solid.

This recipe should be tested using 3/4 c. flour before adding more. If a small round comes up from the broth intact without loosing a lot of the mixture it will hold up while boiling. Simmer for 35 min. or until done. To serve, ladle with slotted spoon onto a platter and drizzle with melted butter. Arrange ham around the dumplings.

The double recipe calls for:
4 c.   potato, ground and drained
2 c.   cubes of bread
1-1/2 t. salt
1   egg
1-1/2 c. flour, test, and add more up to—
1/2 c.   if they don't hold together.

Cold slaw or a large cream dressing salad or sauerkraut is served with this meal. Left over dumplings provide another delicacy the next day, sliced thick and fried in butter till golden.

My Mother's Sauerkraut

Drain 1 qt. sauerkraut, reserve juice; add enough water to cover. In a fry pan, sauté 1/2 lb. bacon halfway through. Drain 1/2 the grease; add 1 lg. chopped onion. Sauté with bacon; add to kraut and —

Add:
1/4 t.	caraway seed
2 T.	brown sugar
1 c.	cabbage, shredded
1 can	mushrooms, drained (sm.)
1	potato, cooked and mashed
some	salt and pepper

Cook on low, heat till tender; adding kraut juice if desired, and to taste.

Josephine Micek
Menomonie, WI

Origin of Noodle Hotdishes

When weather was too dry for crops to grow, the chickens still fared fairly well. They'd scratch all day for seeds and bugs and kept right on laying eggs. When egg prices dropped to 10-cents a dozen, then nine- and even eight-cents, women learned to use them in every imaginable way in their cooking. Besides making the life saving Schmarren (p. 41), noodles were made for soups, or as a maindish with bacon grease or butter poured over, garnished with dry bread croutons, or baked with apples sliced in-between with a bit of butter, sugar and cinnamon added. Out of this was born the yummy hotdishes which became the vogue when the potato crop had dried up.

None of the hotdishes used soups, as in today's recipes, but it didn't delete from the good flavor. So good, in fact, that the recipes are still in use, and are family favorites today. A recipe for extra good noodles follows. These were made so often, even young girls became experts at quickly mixing, rolling ever so thin and cutting them in exactly even strips, ready to hang and dry.

Virginia's Noodles

Beat 6 egg yolks with 6 T. water.
Add: 1 t. salt to approx. 3 c. flour
(Continued on next page)

53

(Continued from last page)

Make a stiff dough. Cut into four pieces. Roll very thin. Let dry on dish towels for a few minutes. Cut into even strips. Hang over the back of a chair which has been covered with a fresh, clean dish towel.

Virginia Clingman
Montevideo MN

The leftover egg whites were used for some of the finest desserts.

Ham Noodle Casserole

Cut lean ham into small cubes and fry in saute pan. Push aside and add flour. Stir to brown gently, using moderate heat. Add cold milk to make a gravy. Season with pepper only. Place in layers in casserole with cooked noodles. Bake till a golden brown. This dish is still popular in Durand, Wisconsin, and the children of this good cook expect it whenever there is a family gathering.

Chicken Noodle Casserole

Cook noodles until tender. Drain and rinse. Melt 1/2 c. margarine, add 1 T. flour, 1 t. salt and 1/4 t. pepper. Stir well. Add 2 c. cold milk slowly and stir till smooth. Alternate noodles, gravy and 3 c. of diced chicken, adding a cup of raw celery if desired. Bake in 350° oven for 1 hr.

My mother was very innovative. One meal I still enjoy was steamed smothered cabbage to which we added cooked elbow macaroni. Any amount of cabbage necessary for helpings needed plus a cup or two of cooked macaroni. I usually also add some onion and celery cut up while smothering the cabbage, adding seasoning to taste. It was interesting to note this recipe appeared in Bon Appetit magazine a while back.

Cecil Johnston
Milwaukee WI

54

CHILDREN HELPING OUT

As children, it was not always understood why parents chose to do things as they did. You just couldn't believe that there wasn't a way for them to buy you that double-dip ice cream cone for five pennies. At least once in a great while. You knew you'd get one at the county fair time IF you got to the fair.

At times distraught parents, coping with their own frustrations, overlooked explanations to their children to ease the feelings. The immediate worries of the parents were never-ending. They dreaded the ominous future which gave no promise of relief. Political rhetoric was just that. Promises of program after program all failed. Parents were engrossed in big problems and real fears of the future.

Olive Jess remembers well the feelings that went with "children helping out," while long-planned dreams were simply forgotten.

My Chicken Project

I was born in 1914 and when I was a little girl of 8 or 9 years old, my parents raised rutabagas to supplement the cow's feed before we had a silo. My father paid each of his 4 children 5-cents a row, but we were eager to earn the money, so we were willing workers.

Often we spent the money we earned on 4th of July firecrackers, but one year I decided to put my money to work to raise more money. I asked my mother for suggestions and she said that I could go down to the neighbors and buy a dozen or so eggs, and I could put them under one of her "setting hens" and raise some Rhode Island Red chickens. Mother's chicken were gray Barred Rocks, so there would be no questions which ones were mine.

How pleased I was as I came home with the Rhode Island Red eggs, and mother helped me put them under a cluck. In a few weeks I had some beautiful little red, fuzzy chicks, which we put in a little house like a doghouse that the folks made especially so the old hen couldn't get out but the little chicks could get out to eat the tender grass shoots. How I fussed with those chicks!

(Continued on next page)

(Continued from last page)

By fall my chicks had grown well, and I helped mother put
them in gunny sacks to take to town to sell. WE also put
her roosters in bags and took them all to town in our
Model T Ford. This day there would be a man there just for
the purpose of buying chickens. I remember he weighed my
chickens separately and I knew how much they were worth.
Mothers roosters brought a lot more because she raised a
lot of chickens.

After we sold our chickens, my folks went to the bank and
to the feed mill, and to the grocery store to buy groceries. They spent all of our chicken money for things that
they bought that day and I never did see one cent of the
money for my chickens. They never mentioned it to me and I
never mentioned it to them. You see, my folks were real
hard up, and I knew that if they were able to give me the
money for my chickens, they would have.

I've often wondered if mother ever felt guilty about not
giving me part of my chicken money. But neither of us ever
mentioned it. Also, I never tried to raise chickens again
— and neither did any of my brothers or sisters.

> Olive Svenson Jess
> Menomonie WI

Your children and grandchildren, I'm sure today, can't
believe half of it. Many times I think it would make
better homemakers, better marriages and less divorces if
things didn't come so easy. Nothing was thrown away, like
now, and we ate what was fixed. We never said "yuk" about
food or we would have been disciplined. Gardening was the
main source of one's living. The whole family worked at
it, too. I'm glad I was brought up in those times, as you
really learn to take care of things and appreciate them. A
product of the Depression.

> Alma Smith
> Woodville WI

Vegetables

These were frugal days but they left us with a happy childhood.

J. Tamse
New Berlin WI

The locusts came in clouds and were so heavy they caused the grain harvest binders to clog up and stall.

Grace Nelson
Beldenville WI

Your book brings back many memories, particularly one of "garlic soup," which consisted of dry bread cubes, minced garlic, a dab of lard and boiling water poured over all.

Lucille Hoolihan
Appleton WI

I recall that we actually mended nylons. I even had a gadget that could take back runs.

Cecil Johnston
Milwaukee WI

Vegetables

Homemakers of the Great Depression depended heavily on their gardens to supply a large amount of their food year around. The best possible use, through canning and preparing fresh vegetable dishes, was made out of everything that grew in the vegetable gardens. Wild greens and berries were not overlooked in supplying many a delicious and nutritious meal.

However, as hard as these times were, they were still to become more difficult. The drought began in 1933 and ravaged on to create the great dust bowl of the century, a climatic disaster. Through this time all crops as well as gardens either dried up or never had ample moisture to germinate seed in the spring. The water table went down so far the wells dried up. Cattle were slaughtered for lack of feed and water to drink. Some were taken to northern Wisconsin where they fed on leaves. And of course, the berry bushes and orchards became casualties as well.

While the gardens grew, before and after the drought but still in the heart of the depression, women prepared generous and delicious meals out of the fruits of the earth. When the climate grew food for the cattle there were dairy products for the table.

We find that cream, eggs, lard, bacon fat and even butter were used in many of the recipes. It has to be remembered that in many homes the little cream they had was sold for cash and could not be used for butter or cream for bread or puddings. Knowing that cream has only 1/3 the calories of mayonnaise, we can in good conscience follow these recipes and enjoy the wholesome goodness of these dishes.

As if times weren't bad enough, all of our potatoes and canned goods were taken by the landlord for past-due rent. That winter we ate cornmeal 3 times a day all winter long.

Anonymous
Ridgeland WI

Ed Sylte worked on a Ridgeland, Wisconsin, farm in Dunn County for his room and board. They had cornmeal for breakfast. It was warmed up for dinner and then it was fried for supper everyday. Eventually Ed upgraded his job by finding a place where meat was served occasionally.

Caring and Sharing

The Frances Olson family of Highland township lived on their grandfather's homesteaded farm not far from the Iowa border. Milo Olson, one of five children was born through the depression. Milo is remembered in this area as the Farm Management Agent of Dunn County in the 1970's.

As a four year old he remembers the time very well. The farm was blessed with a spring which produced cold running water continuously. Over this was built an 8x12 "spring house". It was constructed of limestone and provided them with a place to cool milk and foods in the summer and keep garden produce and food supplies in the winter where they would not freeze.

Fortunately, through the drought the spring also provided water for the vegetable garden. It was 1936 and 1937 that the Olsons were the only family for miles who had a garden. Milo remembers his mother after church asking a neighbor friend how they were getting along. When she learned they had no food at all, Mrs. Olson invited them to dinner. Home from church, Mr. Olson quickly changed his clothes and went out to look over the flock of chickens. He selected the one most likely not to be laying much longer, chopped it's head off, stripped the feathers off and brought it in to Mrs. Olson. By the time the guests arrived they were met by the succulent aroma of a roast chicken dinner with all the trimmings that the times permitted.

Much as they shared, disaster still struck the vegetable garden when the grasshoppers descended like clouds out of the sky. This was almost too much. But Milo remembers the ducks had a holiday. They gulped them up so fast their crops bulged and hung to the ground and they could barely waddle.

Creamed Peas and Potatoes

The first peas and new potatoes from the gardens were always celebrated with this gourmet dish.

Cook:
1 pt.   new peas until just tender. (Do Not overcook)

In a separate pan cook:
4 med.   new potatoes, scraped with chore boy to remove
          skins, and cut in 1" pieces.

Drain vegetables and combine; add 1 pt. light cream brought to a boil with 1 T. cornstarch. Season and serve hot. Parsley or paprika garnish is nice. This can also be thickened by mixing 1 T. flour with 1 T. butter and adding to cream, bring to boil and add to vegetables.

White Sauce

A thin white sauce was sometimes used for the popular spring dish of new potatoes and peas and was almost as easy and quick to make. Thin sauce follows:

Combine: 1 T.   butter
         1 T.   flour

Scald: 1 c.   milk
         1 t.   salt
         1/8 t. pepper

Add to butter mixture; blend well and return to sauce pan and boil gently 1 min.

For medium sauce use 2 T. butter and 2 T. flour.
For thick sauce use 1/4 c. butter and 1/4 c. flour.

This was the basic recipe used for many dishes especially vegetables fresh from the garden.

———

We used to have hot canned tomatoes over mashed potatoes. This was the entire meal — no meat, no milk. The tomatoes and potatoes were grown at home. We also had bean sandwiches, but they were the entire meal. We never had any meat.

Ellen Braun
Minneapolis MN

Hot or Cold String Bean Salad

These were big favorites for perking up any noon or
evening meal. Remember, it was dinner and supper then.

Cook till tender:
1 qt.   green beans, cut into 1 or 2" pieces. Drain.

Slice:
1/2   onion, very thin in rounds and add to beans.

Mix:
4 T.   cream
2 T.   vinegar
1 T.   sugar
some   salt and pepper to taste

Shake well and serve hot or cold.

This dish was generally made in a large batch to serve hot
with the big meal and cold for supper with something else.

Helen J. Cichy
Brandon, MN

Gourmet Golden Squash

Cook squash until tender and drain. Use about 3 lbs.

Mash and stir in:
2 t.   butter
1 c.   sour cream
1/2 c.   grated onion
1 t.   salt
1/4 t.   pepper

Mound in an ungreased casserole. Bake in 400F preheated
oven to heat through.

Creamed Beets

Cook:- 4 or 5 beets until tender, slip skins off and mash coarsely.

Mix:
3 T.	heavy cream
1 T.	vinegar
1 T.	brown sugar
some	salt to taste

Add to beets and mix lightly. Reheat over low fire and serve.

Fried Sweet Corn

Cut sweet corn off 5 cobs.

Melt: 3 T.   butter or margarine in fry pan.

Add: corn and
         1/2 t.   sugar
         3/4 c.   milk

Cover and cook till dry and light golden, watch carefully and stir now and then.

Zora
Sparta, WI

Fried Green Tomatoes

Slice partially ripe tomatoes 1/2" thick. Dip in egg and crackers or pancake mix. They used bread crumbs in the 30's. Fry in bacon fat.

Eva Mae W.
Menomonie, WI

Bacon Cabbage Sauté

Is an excellent side dish which was sometimes almost the entire meal.

Sauté: –
4 strips bacon, until crisp. Break up or cut up before frying.

Measure: –
1/4 c.   pan drippings (or use low cal margarine)
1/2 c.   onions, sauté lightly

Add:–
1 c.   apples, sliced
7-8 c.   cabbage, coarsely cut
1 T.   poppy seed
1 t.   salt
1/4 t.   caraway seed
1/4 c.   cider vinegar

Toss to blend well and cook covered 10 min. Blend in 2 c. cooked egg noodles. Garnish with crumbled bacon and 1/2 c. sour cream.

Creamed Onions

A tasty vegetable that even children enjoy. Onions turn sweet when cooked, like parsnips. Cream adds to the delicate flavor.

Cook: 2 c. sliced onions in small amount of water.

Drain: pour 1 c. cream over and season to taste.

Serve in individual dishes; garnish with paprika.

Potato Puff

Take 2 c. left over mashed potatoes, stir in 2 T. melted butter. Beat and add 2 beaten eggs and 1 c. milk; add salt and pepper, mix well. Bake in casserole for 30 min.

Edna Krebs
Union Grove, WI

64

Tender Beet Tops

Beet tops can be used like spinach and sometimes are preferred. They can be picked fresh from the garden or taken from beets pulled for other uses.

Wash and cook in heavy pan with water clinging to leaves. Sprinkle with salt and cook till wilted and tender; drain. Pour bacon vinegar dressing over and serve hot.

Bacon Vinegar Dressing:

Fry 2 slices of bacon cut into small pieces; add 2 T. vinegar. While hot pour over vegetables; shake in pan and serve.

Larrys' Fresh Corn Pancakes

Cut:- kernels from 3 cobs of corn. Scrape cob to release milk to make 2 c.

In a large bowl stir together:

1 c.	flour	1 T.	sugar
1 t.	baking powder	1 t.	salt
1/8 t.	pepper		

In a small bowl beat together:

2 lg.	eggs	1 c.	milk
2 T.	oil (or melted lard)		

Add to flour mixture; stir to moisten; add corn. Fry small portions in oil till crispy. Serve with maple syrup or breakfast apple sauce. (below)

Breakfast Apple Sauce for French Toast, Pancakes or Waffles

Mix in sauce pan:

1/3 c.	brown sugar
1/2 T.	flour
1/3 c.	water

Add: 2   apples sliced

Cook till it bubbles. Serve hot.

Glenda

65

Bubble and Squeak

Of Irish origin, this dish became popular during the
depression because of it's good taste and available ingredients.

Fry:
3 strips bacon, cut up — remove from pan. Sauté 1 med.
size onion in bacon grease; add 2 c. or more of coarsely
cut up cabbage. Return bacon to pan and stir often. When
cabbage is wilted, add 2 c. left over potatoes. Pat down
to make a large pancake, fry brown on one side, and turn
and brown on other side.

1930's Salad Dressing

Mix together:

1/2 c.	sugar
1 t.	flour
1	egg
1 t.	dry mustard (level)
1/2 t.	salt
1/2 c.	vinegar
1/2 t.	pepper

Cook until thickened.

Hazel Ottman
Elmwood, WI

Cabbage Dressing

1 c.	sugar
1 c.	vinegar

Season with salt and pepper. Cook until it comes to a
boil. Very Good.

—

We lived on vegetables, codfish gravy, johnnie cake, bread
pudding, onion and potato soup, and sidepork gravy. Dessert was always cornstarch pudding, and how I got to hate
it.

Cy Lamb
Chippewa Falls WI

Old Fashioned Cream Dressing

This delightful dressing was used on garden leaf lettuce by the large bowl full as well as on cabbage.

1/2 c.   light cream
1 t.   sugar
1/4 c.   tarragon vinegar (apple cider in 30's)
1/2 t.   salt

Mix and pour over greens, alone or in any combination.

For Egg & Lettuce Salad:

Use a bowl of lettuce torn into small pieces with 2 hard cooked eggs sliced over it. Pour on dressing and toss lightly.

For Cucumbers:

Slice; add salt and let marinate a few minutes. Rinse off and pour dressing over.

Proportions for the same good dressing using sour cream follow:

1-1/2 t. sugar
3/4 c.   sour cream
1 T.   cider vinegar
3/4 t.   salt
dash   pepper

For variation add 1/8 t. mustard.

NOTE: Sour cream dressings have 1/3 the calories of mayonnaise.

Cottage Cheese Dressing

Beat together:-
1/2 c.   milk   1/4 c.   honey or sugar
1/2 t.   salt   1/2 c.   vinegar
3/4 t.   dry mustard   1/2 t.   paprika
1/2 c.   cottage cheese
Dressing may reach desired thickening by chilling. Dab of whipped cream on top of individual plates may top salad.

Elly Kelly
Eau Claire, WI

Sauerkraut

"To make sauerkraut was a job where not only women were needed but also the men. It was a days work. Older children were allowed to stay home from school to run errands or to care for the younger children, while the adults were working.

The crocks were cleaned and air dried the previous season when the Kraut was used up. When it was time to make the sauerkraut again the crocks were freshened up again and the work was begun. The heavy crocks were always kept in the stone walled dark cellar. Lanterns were hung from the rafters when the cellar was in use. The floor of the cellar was tamped earth, generations of feet had made it dust and dirt free. The walls of the cellar were lined with shelves where all the fruit, preserves and pickles were preserves for the long winter. Nothing was wasted. If it was clean and edible, it was somehow preserved and made palatable.

Kraut Making

After the cabbage was cleaned of all soil, it was placed in huge pans where it was rinsed in cool water. Then the large kraut cutter was placed across a suitable tub and cutting began. As the tub filled it was replaced by another, while the cut cabbage was taken down cellar and dumped into the crock. A handful of course canning salt was sprinkled over it and all was stomped down with the stomper. When the crock was filled it was given a final stomping until the juices were released. It was then covered with a clean cloth and the wood cover, which was cut to fit inside the crock, was put into place. A heavy rock of suitable size was washed and placed on top of the wood cover as a weight. The wood cover was made of hardwood, most often out of oak. Another clean cloth covered the entire. Within 12 hrs. fermentation had set in and after 4 to 6 weeks the kraut was ready to use.

During the time of fermentation the scum was removed periodically and the board and rock were washed or rinsed. It was also done each time kraut was removed for use.

(Continued on next page)

Although it involved considerable work, it produced fine sauerkraut providing the vitamin C needed in the diets of that era.

No fruit being available because of lack of refrigeration and no money to buy it, the kraut and tomatoes provided most the vitamin C in the diets."

Helen Cichy
Millerville, MN

Dumplings with Sauerkraut

Cook 1 qt. sauerkraut adding just enough water to barely cover for 20 min.

Mix:
1-1/2 c.   flour, sifted
1 t.   baking powder
1/4 t.   salt
1   egg, beaten
1/4 c.   milk

Cook 5 min. with cover off and 7 min. with cover on.

Corn Pudding

Combine:
1 can   corn
3   egg yolks, beaten
1 T.   sugar
1 T.   cornstarch
1 t.   salt
4 T.   butter, melted

Beat egg whites and fold into mixture. Bake in greased baking dish and bake 30 or 35 min. in 350F oven.

Fresh corn may be used and is very good. 5 or 6 ears replace the pt. of canned corn.

Potato Filling Side Dish

1 c. left over mashed potatoes, mixed with 2 beaten eggs
and 4 slices of cubed bread. Add milk to moisten. Brown
1/3 onion in 2 T. butter and stir into mixture with salt
and pepper. Bake 1 hr. at 375F.

Noodle Apple Side Dish

Layer cooked egg noodles with sliced apples and a small
amount of sugar, cinnamon and dot with butter. Arrange 2
or 3 layers in buttered casserole. Bake till apples are
done.

Dorothy Van Amber
Alexandria, MN

Potato Pancakes

Mix together:
2 c.	grated or ground potatoes
2 T.	flour
1	egg
some	salt and pepper
1 t.	onion, grated

Add enough milk so pancakes spread out nicely in pan. Fry
till brown and crisp. Serve with apple sauce, syrup or
any pancake toppings.

* * *

From Kenosha Wisconsin comes a recipe for an entire meal
in the Sauerkraut pan, save for the mound of mashed
potatoes that goes with this meal.

Gene's Kenosha Kraut

Brown bacon; cut up and drain, 1/2 lb. is just right.
Push bacon to side of pan and add 1 lg. onion, sliced, 3
cloves garlic, chopped, and add 1 lb. fresh cabbage cut
coarsely. Turn lightly to reduce size. Add pepper, no
salt and add 2 lbs. kraut. Stir till hot and bubbly.
Simmer 1 hr. or more; stir to tumble it frequently.

Some cooks added 1/8 t. caraway seed and/or a tart apple.
Serve with lots of whipped potatoes. Brats were served
with this when available. The true Polish cooks broke a
raw egg into the whipped potatoes while beating it.

70

Butchering Day

"Pork hocks, ears and the tails were scrubbed very clean and boiled. Then a vinegar, salt and pepper brine were added to pickle them. Being of Norweigian heritage, nothing was wasted when Dad butchered.

They caught the blood for blood sausage and my aunt came to help. She sewed bags from flour sacks, probably 60 to 100 of them, size 4x10".

They put the blood in dish pans, added barley rice, corn meal or flour and squares of pork fat, enough to thicken it like mush. It was scooped into the bags and tied shut tightly and were stacked in the copper boiler where they were steamed for from 6 to 8 hrs.

We had this for breakfast sometimes, sliced and heated in a pan with milk. We ate this out of a low dish and sprinkled sugar on it. It sounds awful today, but it was very good".

Audrey Samplaski

Easy Jar Kraut

This is an easy recipe for anyone not having a lot of cabbage at one time. It also is not as sour as the crock made cabbage which is why some people like it.

Shred cabbage and pack into qt. or half gal. jars; add 1 t. canning salt as you pack the cabbage in. Pour boiling water over the cabbage with butter knife in jar, cutting around edges to remove all bubbles. Cabbage should not fill jar too high. Pour water off till it's around neck of jar but no cabbage showing. Use zinc lids and rubber seal and cap tightly. Let set at room temp. for 5 or 6 days. If it still bubbles over, remove lid; add salted boiling water and reseal. Store in basement or where it's cool. Edible in 6 weeks.

Some recipes call for 1/2 t. sugar and this makes tasty kraut as well. Do not stomp the cabbage in, just pack it in to fill jar. This will keep as long as water covers the cabbage.

71

Jar Sauerkraut

This recipe adds sugar and is said to be very good.

Slice the cabbage as for kraut. For 1 gal. of kraut mix 4
t. salt and 2 t. sugar. Put this into qt. jars; press
down with wooden spoon till juice comes up and over the
cabbage. Close with rubber ring and zinc cover. Let it
stand in a warm place for a week or two. Then check if
jars are closed tightly and juice covers. If not add
boiling salted water and close lids again. Store in cool
dark place.

Lila J.
Germany

Another Good Jar Kraut

Easy to make and always good, this kraut can be put up a
jar at a time or whenever a head of cabbage is ready.

Shred cabbage fine. Pack into sterile jars leaving inch
or more from top. Add 1 t. salt and 1 t. sugar; pour
boiling water over. Seal tight with zinc cover and let
stand at room temp. for 2 weeks. If juice runs over and
bubbles out unscrew lid; add boiling salted water and
reseal.

* * *

When they say the good old days they must have forgotten
how hard we worked. Although as we look back we enjoyed
it too.

The chickens just ran around and picked for themselves. I
don't know if there was such a thing as buying chicken
feed. The hens would "set" and we'd have a batch of
little ones.

Audrey Samplaski

In some localities, sauerkraut was kept in crocks on the
porch in the wintertime. Portions were hacked off and
used. Anything left in spring was canned by the hot water
method.

72

"I remember the "Depression" very well. We were a family of twelve children so all had to help. I don't know how my mother endured it all, but she did. She died five years ago at 92 years plus.

Dad and my brothers enjoyed hunting. We seldom had beef because we needed the cows for milk and the steer calves were sold. Once in a while we had mutton because we had sheep — and bees for honey.

Mom always raised a <u>big</u> garden in addition to the field of sweet corn, cucumbers, squash, green and yellow beans and strawberries. We raised the beans and cucumbers for the factory. That was how we earned a little money for our 4th of July firecrackers and school clothes. You can bet we didn't spend too much on firecrackers.

During the worst of the depression two married daughters returned home with their husbands and babies. We had people sleeping in the living room, a bunk house in summer and there was even an extra double bed in my parents bedroom. And there were often guests for mealtime. My parents never sent anyone away hungry and tired — even if they had to sleep in the hay mow. It seemed that every itinerant salesman, horse trader and tramp arrived at our house at mealtime."

Julie Weiss
Mondovi

Howard Helgeson of Ridgeland, Wisconsin, has a special touch with his Butterfly Venison Tenderloin. He brushes them with butter and charcoals them on the grill, turning occasionally and brushing with butter each time.

His cream-fried squirrel is a special dish as well.

Cream-Fried Squirrel

Soak pieces in salt water; drain. Add fresh water and boil until tender. Fry in heavy cream and season to taste.

Antelope Roast

Line bottom of roasting pan with bacon. Place antelope roast on bacon and roast 1-1/2 to 2 hrs. at 250°. Baste occasionally. No other seasoning is needed.

CHILD ONCE HAPPY WITH ONLY A DOLL

The 1938 Montgomery Ward's Christmas catalog arrived at our farm home. As I paged through it for the umpteenth time, I asked, "Mama, do you think I could have a new doll?"

"Well," she answered thoughtfully, "you know you can't expect a new doll every year. Besides, you have nice dolls."

Yes, it was true that I had two dolls. One was a Shirley Temple doll who had long ago lost her blonde curls. The other one was a Betsy Wetsy doll with a very offensive odor because of too many little bottles of water poured through her rubber body.

Being six years old, I had begun to realize that Santa had to have considerable help from Mama and Papa. I was born in the midst of the Great Depression and six years later the cream check didn't cover much more than basic needs.

Two weeks before Christmas our parents took my brother and me to Menomonie to see the Christmas decorations and toys. As we went from Farmer's Store to Wards and down to the Gambles store, Mama watched as I longingly wished for one of the new dolls.

Christmas Eve day arrived. The parlor to our country home was "shutoff" all winter except for Christmas. Papa lit a fire in the big Heatrola stove before he went to the barn to do chores that evening. When the chores were done, we went to Christmas Eve service at church.

After returning home, Mama carried the Aladdin lamp into the warm parlor. There in the soft lamplight I saw the most beautiful doll in all the world. She had real hair with brown ringlets that hung to her waist. Sitting in a doll highchair, she wore a bright red dress with a beautiful lace ruffle around the collar.

Oh how lovingly I picked her up and chattered about my new doll. After a few minutes Mama smilingly asked, "Honey, don't you recognize your doll?"

I held the doll's face to mine. Her soft brown eyes began to sparkle as her white teeth smiled and her dimples deepened.

"Mama!" I shouted, "this is my Shirley Temple doll." I saw
Papa wink and they smiled knowing their ingenuity had paid
off. A $1.98 doll wig from the Montgomery Ward catalog, a
few scraps of material and some lace and some odd pieces
of wood had made their little girl the happiest girl in
Dunn County.

This doll still occupies a prominent place in my home.
Both of us have a few extra creases in our face, our eyes
aren't as bright and our cheeks aren't as rosy as they
once were. But this Christmas as I hold her, we'll smile
at each other and remember a Christmas almost 50 years ago
when happiness was a recycled Shirley Temple doll.

                    Joyce Solie
                    Menomonie WI

Etta M. Wiseman of Eau Claire WI walked the entire city
over and called on each merchant daily asking for a job.
In six weeks she was asked to report to work at 50-cents a
day. She recalls being absolutely delighted at her good
fortune.

MY FAMILY TREASURY OF HEIRLOOM RECIPES

Date Recorded_____

Cakes, Pies, Cookies

CAKES, PIES AND COOKIES

Plain White Sugar Cookies

This is a tried and true recipe dating back long before the Depression of the 1930's. It survived that period because most homes had the simple ingredients the recipe calls for. It was always made at Christmastime, and even today is traditional in many homes.

Mix: 1 c. butter
     3 c. flour as for pie crust; set aside

Break two eggs into a bowl and beat.

Add: 1 c. sugar
     3 T. milk
     1 t. baking soda and mix well

Add: 1/2 t. vanilla
     1/2 t. lemon extract

Some nutmeg may be added.

Add the above to the flour mixture and mix well. Roll out thin and bake at 375° until golden. Do not bake too long. This recipe is the least work for rolled cookies and they are rich enough to be very tasty.

From Iris Martin of Sheboygan WI comes this cherished cake recipe found by her when she was a Girl Scout in 1930. The cream used in the topping was skimmed off the quart milk bottle which was not homogenized as today's milk is.

Lazy Daisy Cake

Beat two eggs; gradually add 1 c. sugar. Sift together 1 c. flour, 1/4 t. salt, 1 t. baking powder. Fold into egg mixture. Boil together 1/2 c. milk, 1 T. butter; then add 1 t. vanilla. Mix carefully into the above. Batter will be thin. Bake at 325™ for 25-30 min. After baking, spread with icing as follows while cake is still warm: 5 T. butter, 10 T. brown sugar, 4 T. cream and 1 c. coconut. Brown under broiler.

Mother's Apron

Do you remember Mother's Aprons? Always big, they were, and their uses myriad. Besides, the foremost purpose, the protection of the dress beneath, it was a holder for removing pot and pans from the oven, it was wonderful for drying children's tears and, yes, even for wiping small noses and shooing flies.

From the hen house it carried eggs, fuzzy chicks, ducklings or goslings, — sometimes half hatched eggs to be finished in the warming oven. It's folds provided an ideal hiding place for shy children and when guests lingered on chilly days, the apron was wrapped around mother's arms.

Innumerable times it wiped a perspiring brow bent over a hot, wood burning stove. Chips and kindling came to the kitchen stove in the ample garment, as did fresh peas and string beans from the garden — often they were podded and stemmed in the lap the apron covered. Windfall apples, kindling chips and corn cobs were gathered in it, and wild flowers.

Chairs were hastily dusted with its corners when unexpected company was sighted. Waving it aloft was as good as a dinner bell to call the men from the fields. Big, they were. Yes, and useful. Now, I'm wondering —— will any modern, frilled plastic apron provoke such nostalgic memories?

A Listener

Tune to WRFW 10—10:15

This is Elly Kelly saying: "Be pleasant until 10:00 o'-clock in the morning and the rest of the day will take care of itself".

"I can remember the first place that Jack took me when I met Jack - to the famous Fish House in Winona, MN. and the highest price meal was 67 cents.

"My father was a grocer. He took cords of wood from farmers for groceries. The good old days; I loved them".

Elly Kelly of Eau Claire, WI

Eggless, Milkless, Butterless Cake

This Moravian, Czechoslovakian cake somehow found it's way to the United States with the valued possessions of immigrant women.

It was so popular in Wisconsin during the depression one would have thought it was invented there.

The recipes varied, but one can almost be sure the Wisconsin ladies made it the best. The following comes from the kitchen of Fairy Holm, Eau Claire, Wisconsin, and it is delicious. Almost like an apple sauce cake, spicy, fruity and moist.

Boil 5 min. and cool:
2 c.	sugar
2 c.	raisins
2 c.	water
2 T.	lard

Add: 1 T.   molasses

Sift:
1 t.	soda	1 t.	nutmeg
1 t.	allspice	3 c.	flour

Add: - to above. Mix and bake in 8" square pan at 350F for 35 min. or toothpick test. Variations were many from:-

* * *

Lorna Kindermann, Eau Claire, Wisconsin makes a good one adding nuts as follows:

1 c.   brown sugar — boil together with
1-1/4 c. water
1 c.   raisins
1/3 c.   shortening — cool 3 min.

Add:- Sifted together
2 c.	flour
3 t.	baking powder
1 t.	nutmeg
1 t.	cinnamon
1/2 t.	salt

Mix well and add 3/4 c. chopped nuts. Bake in moderat' oven 45 min.

Christine Granger Klatt from Menomonie calls her cake a Raisin Spice Cake. Hers calls for 1 t. baking powder and 1 t. soda. She adds two eggs to hers and bakes it 1 hr. in a med. size pan. The rest of the ingredients are as above.

Others with variations sent in recipes from:

Elmwood, WI   Lois Littlefield
Elmwood, WI   Hazel Ottman
Holcombe, WI   Betty Ewer
Chippewa Falls, WI   Linda Weber

and still others.

Applesauce Cake

Cream: 1/2 c.   shortening
          1 c.   brown sugar

Add: 1 c.   applesauce

Sift: 2-1/4 c.   flour
         1/2 t.   soda
         1/2 t.   salt
         1 t.   baking powder
         1/2 t.   cinnamon

Gradually beat into sugar mixture. Add:- 1 c. chopped walnuts. Pour into med. size pan 8-1/2x4-1/2x2-1/2" or similar. Bake 1 hr. at 325F. Frost as you please.

Christine Granger Klatt
Menomonie, WI

The delicious Caramel Frosting comes from Christine as well:

Mix in sauce pan:-   2 T.   butter or margarine
                        1/3 c.   milk
                        2/3 c.   brown sugar

Bring to a boil stirring constantly. Remove from heat, add vanilla and enough powdered sugar for good spreading consistency.

Corn Syrup Sponge Cake

Separate 4 eggs. Beat whites with 1/4 t. salt until stiff, but not dry. Heat 3/4 c. white corn syrup to boiling and pour slowly over whites beating constantly. Add grated rind of 1/2 lemon to egg yolks; beat till thick and lemon colored. Fold into first mixture. Sift 1 c. flour with 1/2 t. baking powder; fold into egg mixture. Pour into 9" tube pan, ungreased. Bake at 325F for about 50 min.

Lois Littlefield
Elmwood, WI

Soft Ginger Cake

Combine: 1/2 c.   sugar   1 c.   molasses

Add: 1/2 c.   butter — and mix well.

Dissolve: 2 t.   soda — in   ] Add, to first
          1 c.   boiling water   ] mixture.

Sift: 2-1/2 c. flour — with pinch of salt
          1 t.   ginger
          1 t.   cinnamon
          1/4 t.   cloves

Add to molasses mixture and beat. Add 2 beaten eggs last. Bake at 350F for 25 to 35 min. This is an excellent cake served with whipped cream.

From collection of   Velma Lillian Fenske
                            Menomonie, WI
Also from   Lois Littlefield
with variation   Elmwood, WI

Sour Milk Spice Cake

Cream: 1/2 c. shortening   1 c.   sugar

Add: 1   egg

Dissolve: 1 t.   soda — in
          1 c.   sour milk or buttermilk

Add alternately with:

2 c.	flour, sifted
1 t.	cloves (heaping)
1 t.	cinnamon
1/2 t.	nutmeg
1/4 t.	salt

Bake at 350F for 25 or 30 min. Toothpick test.

Frost with: 1/2 c.   white sugar
             1 c.   brown sugar
             1/2 c.   cream

Boil till soft ball stage. Cool slightly. Beat till spreading consistency. If it gets a bit too hard, add a few drops of cream.

This cake was stirred up in a few minutes rarely using a recipe, and served with or without icing, hot and fresh. Whipped cream was excellent with it.

1937 Violet Prestegard

Sorghum Cake (Depression Cake)

Mix: 1/2 c. sugar   1/2 c.   lard

Add: 2   eggs
      1/2 c.   sorghum   1/2 c.   sour milk

Sift: 2 c.   flour — with   1 t.   soda
       1/2 t.   baking powder   1 t.   salt
       1 t.   cinnamon   1/2 t.   ginger

Add to the above and bake in moderate oven until done. This is similar to a recipe using honey in place of the sorghum.

Vera Lindsay
Mondovi, WI

Dutch Apple Cake

Mix:-
2 c.   flour, sifted
1/2 t.   salt
3 t.   baking powder

Cut in:-
1/4 c.   butter — mixing well.

Beat:
1   egg — and add to
1 c.   milk (scant)

Stir in dry mixture. Dough should be soft enough to
spread 1/2" thick in shallow pan. Core and peel 4 or 5
apples and cut into 1/8ths. Lay slices parallel on top of
dough, sharp edge down, and press into dough. Sprinkle 2
T. sugar on apples. (Some recipes call for cinnamon also)
Bake in hot oven 20 to 30 min. Serve hot with butter or
with lemon sauce as a pudding.

> Lorna Kindermann
> Eau Claire, WI

Eggless 3 Layer Cake

Stir butter the size of an egg (1/3 c.) with 1 c. sugar
mixing very well. Pour in 1 c. sour milk, do not stir.

Sift: 2 c.   flour
          1/2 t.   soda
          1-1/4 t. baking powder
          2 T.   cornstarch

Add to above mixture and beat thoroughly. Add:- 1 t.
lemon extract. Bake in 3 layers, at 325F for 20 min. or
till done. Put some nice tart jelly between layers and
you will have an inexpensive delicious cake.

> Lois Littlefield
> Elmwood, WI

A similar recipe called for serving this cake with whipped
cream.

Quick Strawberry Preserve Frosting

Combine: 1   egg white
        1/8 t.   salt
        1 c.   strawberry perserves

Beat till frosting stands in peaks.

Ellen Johnson
Elk Mound, WI

A later version calls for 1/4 c. powdered milk (Sanalac) added while beating (not milk granules). Or folding in whipped cream for a gourmet touch.

Wedding Cake

And also for a royal birthday, this exquisite cake adorned the center of the table at many gala celebrations. The frosting or icing is a sugar saver which complimented the cake, especially since 2 c. were used for the batter.

Ice Cream Cake

Also called Cornstarch Cake

Cream: 2 c.   sugar
       3/4 c.   butter — until fluffy

Sift: 2 c.   flour, sifted
       1 c.   cornstarch
       3 t.   baking powder

Add alternately with: 1 c.   milk
                           dash   salt

Add: some   vanilla or almond extract

Beat: 5 egg whites, till stiff but not dry.
        Fold in carefully.

Bake in layer cake pans for 25 min. or until toothpick comes out clean. Oven at 350F.

Frosting

For wedding or birthday cake.

Mix: 2 T.   flour
           1/2 c. sugar

Add: 1/2 c. milk

Blend well and cook till thick; stir and cool.

Beat in: 1/2 c. shortening
        1/4 t. salt
        1 c.   powdered sugar
        some   flavoring

Beat very well till light and fluffy. Can be colored as desired.

Dorothy Van Amber
Alexandria, MN

Ornamental Icing

2 c. powdered sugar   3/4 c. Crisco
1/4 t. cream of tartar   dash salt

Beat well. Dip spoon in water occasionally; add flavoring.

D. Van Amber

Dolores' Apple Cake

Beat 3 eggs until thick and lemon-colored.
Add: 1-3/4 c. sugar
    1 t.   vanilla
—along with:
    2 c.   sifted flour
    1 t.   cinnamon
    1 t.   baking soda
    1 c.   vegetable oil
    2   apples, sliced and unpeeled
    1/3 c. nuts
Bake at 350° for 1 hr., or until done. Sprinkle with powdered sugar.

D.C. Stensrud
Brandon MN

Overnight Birthday Cake

This is a cake for special occasions and is very delicious. When cake flour was not available scant 1/2 c. cornstarch was used in place of part of the flour.

2 c.	cake flour
2 c.	white sugar
1 c.	boiling water

Mix together and let stand overnight. In morning stir thoroughly.

Beat: 6   egg whites — stiff

Add: 1 t.   cream of tartar
       2 t.   baking powder
       1 t.   flavoring

Fold into mixture. Bake at 250F for 35 min.

Dorothy Van Amber
Alexandria, MN

Salted Peanut Birthday Cake

Cream: 1 c.   sugar
        1/3 c.   lard

Add: 1 lg.   egg
        1 c.   thick sour milk

Sift: 1-3/4 c. flour
        1 t.   soda

Add: 1 c.   ground salted peanuts with red skins.

Mix well into above mixture. Bake in 9x12" pan at 350F for 35 min. Frost with white frosting; sprinkle top with peanuts (crushed).

Velma Fenske collection
Menomonie, WI

Never Fail White Cake

Cream together: 1-1/2 c. sugar
                     1/2 c. butter

Add: 1 c.   sweet milk with
         2 c.   flour
         2 t.   baking powder
         1 t.   vanilla

Fold in stiffly beaten whites of 4 eggs. Bake in moderate oven. Toothpick test, or 25 min. approximately.

Betty Ewer
Holcombe, WI

Glenn's Favorite Chocolate Cake

Mix: 2/3 c.   shortening
        1-3/4 c. sugar

Add: 1-1/4 c. milk
        1-1/2 t. soda added

Sift: 1-3/4 c. flour
        2/3 c.   cocoa
        1/2 t.   cream of tartar
        1/2 t.   salt

Add to above and beat. Add 3 eggs and mix well. Bake at 350F for about 30 min.

Dorothy Van Amber
Alexandria, MN

Soft Chocolate Frosting

Melt:- 6 oz. chocolate in saucepan over hot water.
Beat:- 3 egg yolks in heavy saucepan until very thick.
Add:- 1-1/4 c. sugar and beat till smooth.
Add:- 3/4 c. milk and 1-1/2 T. butter or margarine, stirring well.

Cook over very low heat, stirring constantly. Bring to a boil and boil 1 min. only. Remove from heat. Stir in chocolate; add salt and vanilla. Beat until of spreading consistency. This icing stays soft and is sufficient for a large pan cake.

Gum Drop Fruit Cake

Cream: 2 c.   lard, melted
           1 c.   sugar
           1 c.   brown sugar

Add: 4   eggs, beaten
           2 c.   unsweetened apple sauce

Sift: 4-1/2 to 5 c. flour with 2 t. soda and 1/4 t. salt.

Add: 1 c.   dates, cut in 1/2
           1 c.   Brazil nuts, cut in 1/2
           1 c.   small gum drops (no blacks or spiced)
           1 c.   raisins, soaked
           2 t.   cinnamon
           2 t.   nutmeg
           2 t.   allspice

Mix well and bake in 3 bread tins at 350F for 45 min. This is another very good old recipe always used at Christmas time.

V.L. Fenske

Biscuit Short Cake

Sift and measure 3 c. flour. Sift with 3 T. sugar, 4 t. baking powder and 1/2 t. salt. Cut in 6 T. shortening and 2 T. butter. Add 1 c. milk and mix lightly. Turn out on floured board; knead gently. Pat in sheet 1/4" thick; cut with floured cutter. Spread 1/2 the biscuit with butter. Place unbuttered biscuit on buttered one. Bake at 450F for 15 min. Split and ladle crushed berries (sweetened) between and over biscuits. Serve with whipped cream.

Delores Papenfus
Mondovi, WI

Orange Loaf

This recipe is later than the 1930's but is such a favorite with this family it deserves inclusion.

Place in a bowl:
1/2 c.	orange juice
some	grated rind of one orange
1/2 c.	boiling water
3/4 c.	raisins

Add:
1 c.	sugar	]
1 t.	soda	] Mix
2 T.	butter	] well.
2 t.	vanilla	]
1	egg, beaten	]

Add:
2 c.	flour
1/2 t.	baking powder
1/4 t.	salt
1/2 c.	nuts, chopped

Bake at 350F for 1 hr. Ice with thin powdered sugar icing if desired.

Paula Collins
Eau Claire, WI

Raised Doughnuts

This Sunday afternoon depression treat was made occasionally when there was a day for celebration. Almost all of them were eaten fresh and warm. Neighbors were invited in for this and the large coffee pot was put on the fire.

Soften: 1 cake yeast in — 1/4 c. lukewarm water

Mix and add:
1 c.	milk
3 T.	sugar
1 t.	salt
2 T.	butter
2	eggs, beaten
1/2 t.	cinnamon

Add: 2 c. flour and let rise. Beat down and add 2 more c. flour. Pat out on floured board. Cut out and let rise again. Fry till brown in hot fat; sprinkle with sugar.

90

Drop Doughnut Balls

Another good school lunch item was popular with field lunches as well.

Mix: 1/3 c.   sugar
            1/2 c.   milk
            1   egg

Add: 2 T.   shortening, melted

Sift: 1-1/2 c. flour
           3/4 T.   salt
           2 T.   baking powder
           1/2 T.   cinnamon

Add to liquid and mix lightly. Drop by t. into hot 375F fat till brown. Dust with powdered sugar. Makes 3 dozen.

Dorothy Van Amber
Alexandria, MN

Green Tomato Mincemeat

1 pt.   green tomatoes, chopped
1-1/2 pt. apples, chopped
1 lb.   raisins, chopped

Add: 3 c.   sugar
           2 t.   cinnamon
           1 t.each salt, allspice, cloves
           1/4 c.   vinegar

Cook until thick; can and seal. This can be frozen. No meat in this one but an all time favorite with many families today. A must for the Amery, Wisconsin deer hunters.

Dorothy Van Amber
Alexandria, MN

Wonderful Mince Meat

Boil: 3 lbs. beef till tender. Leave in water to cool, then chop small pieces.

Add:
1 lb.	suet, chopped
1/2 lb.	citron
3 lbs.	seeded raisins
2 lbs.	currants
1 lb.	walnuts
6 lbs.	apples
3 T.	cinnamon
1 T.	cloves
1 t.	pepper
2 T.	salt
5 lbs.	light brown sugar
2 qts.	cider vinegar

Cook in heavy cooking vessel 1 hr. watching very carefully to avoid burning. This makes 11 qts. of very delicious mince meat. It should be canned.

Berends
Clark County

Million Dollar Cookies

Everyone made these cookies. Even the kids could mix them up and have them ready for the next day's school lunch.

1 c.	shortening
1/2 c.	brown sugar
1/2 c.	white sugar — mix together and add
1	egg
1 t.	vanilla — mix and add
2 c.	flour, sifted — with
1/4 t.	soda
1/2 t.	salt
1/2 c.	nuts — if available.

Drop from spoon and bake till light golden.

Snickerdoodles

This is a version of the million dollar cookie with slightly different proportions and method.

Cream:
3/4 c.   shortening
1-1/2 c. sugar

Add:
2   eggs

Sift together:
2-3/4 c. flour
1 t.   soda
1 t.   cream of tartar
1/2 t.   salt

Mix and chill. Roll in balls and dip in mixture of 2 T. sugar and 2 t. cinnamon. Bake at 350F till light golden.

Ginger Creams

Cream together:
1/2 c.   shortening
1 c.   sugar

Add:
1 c.   sweet or sour cream
2   eggs
1/2 c.   molasses
pinch   salt

Mix and add:
3-1/2 c. flour, sifted
2 t.   soda
1 t.   cinnamon
1 t.   ginger

Add nuts and raisins if desired. Spread on bottom of pan quite thin. Bake in moderate (350F) oven 20-25 min., or till toothpick tests done. Ice with thin powdered sugar icing.

Mary Ann
Benson, MN

"Another food that stretched our menu was cracklings. This is the fat left over after the fat is rendered. The fried fat was put into a press, the lard squeezed out and the left over product was called "cracklings". These were salted slightly and stored in a container for future use.

The cracklings would be put into the oven to heat thoroughly and would generally be served with rye bread or boiled potatoes. Other times they would be mixed with flour and baked on a cookie sheet and be eaten as a bread substitute".

Marie Larson
Rice Lake, WI

Crackling Cookies

The cracklings are the by-product of rendered lard. Even though they are not common today this recipe is so true — Depression that it must be included.

2 c.	crackling		
1 c.	brown sugar		
1 c.	white sugar		
2	eggs		
1/2 c.	milk		
4 c.	flour, sifted with —		
2 t.	baking powder	1 t.	soda
1 t.	salt	1 t.	vanilla
1 t.	nutmeg	1 t.	cinnamon
1 t.	cloves	1 c.	raisins
1 c.	nuts		

Bake at 350F until light brown. Do not overbake.

Audrey Samplawski
Chetek, WI

Sour Cream Sugar Cookies

This delicious cookie recipe is very old but it survived the Great Depression and still is used today. Easy to mix and quick to roll out and bake, the recipe makes 75 great tasting cookies.

1 c.	margarine or butter	2 c.	sugar
1 c.	sour cream	3	eggs
5 c.	flour	4 t.	baking powder
1 t.	soda	1 t.	salt
1/2 t.	cream of tartar	1 T.	vanilla

Mix and rest overnight in refrigerator. Roll dough out and before cutting sprinkle with sugar. Bake at 325F till very light golden.

Christine Klatt
Menomonie, WI

Country Crisp Sugar Cookies

This recipe calls for rolling out the dough after chilling overnight. It can also be rolled into shape and sliced the next day for easier and quicker cookie baking.

It was said no Christmas was complete without sugar and molasses cookies.

This recipe was the old standby which was also used year around.

Cream: 1/2 c. butter or margarine
        1 c.   sugar — till light and fluffy.

Add: 1   egg
        1 T.   cream
        1 t.   vanilla — beat well.

Sift: 2 c.   flour
        1 t.   baking powder
        1/2 t. salt

Add to creamed mixture beating until well combined. Chill overnight. Can be rolled and cut out or formed into a roll and sliced the next day or when ready to use. Sprinkle with sugar before baking. Bake for 5 min. or until very light golden.

95

Economy Bars

Cream: 1 c.   butter
           1 c.   brown sugar

Add: 2 c.   dry oatmeal   ] Put half
           2 c.   flour   ] in greased
           1 t.   baking powder] bar pan.

Add: 1 c.   sugar
           1 c.   water
           1 lb.   dates — cooked to thick paste,
                     stirring often.

Pour over mixture in pan and add the rest of the flour mixture crumbles on top. Bake in a moderate oven for 20 min. or till light brown on top. These were made with commodity raisins in the 1930's, and were also very good.

Clarice Personius
Jordan, MN

Raisin Bars

Boil: 1 c.   raisins
           2 c.   water — for 10 min.

Add: 1/2 c. shortening — and cool well

Add: 1 c.   sugar   1-3/4 c. flour
     1 t.   soda   some   cinnamon and nutmeg

Bake at 350F for about 25 min. Frost with the following:

1 c.   brown sugar   1/2 c. white sugar
2 T.   butter   1/3 c. milk

Mix and boil to soft ball stage. Beat and spread. Dilute with a bit of milk if it gets too thick.

The government gave raisins and other foods to families that qualified to help the hungry masses of people. They were called commodities. Raisins were used in everything baked it seems or stewed. Dates can be used in these recipes to replace the raisins for a variation, except in the raisin pies.

School Lunch Chocolate Drop Cookie

Melt: 1/2 c.   butter — with
            2/3 c.   cocoa
                   (lard was used in the 30's)

Add to: 1 c.   sugar
          1 c.   sour milk (milk with vinegar is good sub.)

Add: 1/2 t.   salt
          1 t.   baking powder
          1 t.   soda
          1 c.   nuts (when available)
          2 c.   flour

Mix and drop from t. on greased cookie sheet. Bake at
350F for 8 to 10 min. Do not overbake. Hazel nuts were
gathered by the sackful in the late summers. They were
dried in the sun and the outer shells were removed. Ten
gunny sacks full provided a household with 100 lbs. of
nuts. Nuts were used as nourishment and replaced the
usual popcorn every now and then for an evening of treats,
as well as for baking and for all the puddings that were
made.

Dorothy's Never Fail Pie Crust

Mix: 3 c.   flour
        1-1/4 c. shortening

Add: 1   egg, beaten   1 T.   vinegar
        5 T.   water   1/4 t.   salt

Makes 4 bottoms.

Rhubarb Custard Pie

Art's favorite

Mix: 1-3/4 c. sugar
        3 T.   flour
        1/4 t.   cinnamon
        3   eggs, well beaten

Pour over 3 c. rhubarb cut fine in unbaked pie shell.
Bake at 350F until custard is done.

Rhubarb Custard Pie with Cream

Fill unbaked pie crust 1/2 full of cut up rhubarb.
Sprinkle with 1/2 c. sugar.

Make custard of:

1 c.	white syrup
4 T.	sugar
1 c.	cream
3	eggs
1-1/2 t.	cornstarch

Pour over rhubarb and bake till done. Clean knife test.

Raisin Sour Cream Pie

Mix and cook until it begins to thicken:

1 c.	sour cream	2 T.	cornstarch
1/2 t.	salt	1/3 c.	sugar
1-1/2 t.	cinnamon		

Add: 2   egg yolks
        1/3 c.   milk

Cook about 2 min. Fold in 1 c. raisins which have been
rinsed and soaked in hot water and towel dried. Make
meringue out of egg whites and bake for 30 min. or until
nicely browned.

Buttermilk Pie

Make a pastry for one crust pie and coat inside with egg
white.

Beat together: 2 eggs   and   1 t. cinnamon

Mix: 1 T. flour   and   1/2 c.   sugar

Stir in: 1 c.   buttermilk

Add: to egg mixture, stir well and pour into pastry shell.
Bake at 450F for 10 min. Reduce heat and bake at 350F for
another 30 min.
Sugar can be replaced with 1/3 c. Karo syrup. Sour milk
may be used as well and makes a very nice pie.

H.J.C.
Brandon, MN

Prize Winning Pecan Pie

Line 9" pie pan with pastry.

Mix together:
2		eggs, beaten
1 c.		syrup
1/8 t.		salt
1 t.		vanilla
3/4 c.		sugar (1/2 can be used)
2 T.		butter, melted

Add last: 1 c.   pecan meats whole

Pour into pastry shell and bake on 400F for 15 min. and on 350F for 30 min. longer or till knife comes out clean.

This recipe has been used for peanut pie, butternut pie, walnut pie and wild hazel nut pie. Some restaurants are famous for this recipe made with peanuts, slightly crushed, or using walnuts.

A modern day version called "Sinfully Delicious", is made by adding 1/3 c. cocoa to the sugar and proceeding as above. Whipped cream is served with this.

Sugarless Molasses Cookies

1-1/2 c. dark molasses
3/4 c.   shortening
1/3 c.   boiling water — poured over above.
2   egg, beaten — mix well.

Add:
4 c.   flour — sifted with
2 t.   soda
2 t.   salt
1/4 t.   ginger
1 t.   cinnamon

Mix and chill overnight. Slice and bake at 350F for 8 to 10 min. Makes 3 dozen.

This is another school lunch treat everyone enjoyed.

Del F.

Christmas Cookies

We made these by the bushel full and stored them in crocks covered with a large plate and stored in the back of the cupboard. We started making these right after Thanksgiving because they improved with age.

They were frosted with the seven minute icing which follows which stayed nice indefinitely.

Bring to a boil: 2 c.   molasses
                     1 c.   syrup

Pour over: 1-1/2 c. lard

Let cool and add: 10 T.   water
                     1 t.   salt

Add: 1-1/2 c. sugar   1 t.   ginger
     1 t.   cinnamon   1/2 t. allspice
     1/2 t. nutmeg

Sifted with: 4 t.   soda
                     4 c.   flour

Mix well. Add more flour till right consistency to roll. Cut in shapes and bake. Cool and frost.

Cookie Icing for Christmas Cookie

In top of double boiler combine:
2   egg whites
1/2 c.   light corn syrup
1/2 c.   sugar
1/8 t.   salt

Beat till mixed. Set over boiling water and beat till it stands in peaks. Remove from stove and add 1 t. vanilla; beat one min. more. Add 1 T. butter and 1 T. flour. Beat well. Frost cookies and let them dry before storing, so they don't stick together.

Use also on the cookies that follow.

Depression Cookies

Combine:

1 c.	sugar		1 c. -	lard
1 c.	molasses		1 c.	boiling water

Add: 4-1/2 c. flour — to which has been added:-

1 t.	ginger
1 t.	cinnamon
1 t.	soda
no	eggs

Let stand for 1 hr. in cool place. Roll out quite thick. Cut and bake at 375F for 10 min. Frost with the above icing or sprinkle with sugar before baking.

Ginger Snap Cookie

This 75 year old recipe had never lost it's popularity. Similar to the Christmas molasses cookie, ingredients very only slightly, and dough is rolled into walnut size, dipped in sugar and flattened with a glass. If cookies do not crack on top add a bit more flour. Use method as for Christmas cookie.

2 c.	sugar
1 c.	molasses
2	eggs
1 c.	lard (Do not substitute)
3 t.	soda (rounding)
4-1/2 c.	flour — sifted with
1/4 t.	salt
1 t.	cinnamon
2 t.	ginger
1/2 t.	cloves
1 t.	vanilla

Bake at 350F for 8 to 10 min. Aging improves this cookie. Very good with a fresh hot cup of coffee and a chat with a friend, it is said.

From the collection of   Velma L. Fenske
Menomonie, WI

Old Fashioned Soft Molasses Cookie

Dated 1927, this is a delicious soft cookie often quickly made to send out to the threshing crew. They never have a chance to get old.

Cream: 1 c.   sugar
         1 c.   lard

Add: 1 c.   molasses — mix

Add: 2 c.   flour — sifted with
         1 t.   ginger
         2 t.   soda
         1/2 t. cloves
         1/4 t. salt

Add alternately with 1 c. cold water. Add up to 1-1/2 c. more flour or stiff enough to handle. Roll in walnut size; dip in sugar and bake in moderate oven for 8 to 10 min.

Hazel Ottman
Elmwood, WI

Apples!   Apples!   Apples!

They did more with the Big Apple than dance it. They ate it. In every manner shape and form.

Applesauce

Wash, pare, quarter and core 8 juicy apples. Add 1/2 c. water and cook in heavy sauce pan covered until tender. Add 3/4 c. sugar and cook a few min. longer. Serves six. Cloves, cinnamon or nutmeg may be added.

Apple Pie

Line 9" tin with pastry.

Mix:
1 c.	sugar	1/2 t.	ginger
1 t.	cinnamon	1/4 t.	nutmeg
1/4 t.	salt	2 T.	flour
1 T.	lemon juice		

Fill pastry with alternate layers of 4 c. sliced apples and above mixture. Heap slightly. Dot with butter. Add top crust. Bake 40 or 50 min. or until apples are done and crust is brown.

Apple Crisp

Slice 4 c. apples and place in buttered pan. Sprinkle with 1 T. cinnamon and 1/2 t. salt.

Blend:
3/4 c.	flour	1 c.	sugar
1/3 c.	butter		

Sprinkle over all. Bake at 350F for 40 min. Serve hot or cold with cream or whipped cream.

Jan Paske

Oatmeal Crisp

This variation was just as popular as the above. Oatmeal was used extensively because it was cheap and filling. It is also very nutritious.

4 c.	apples	1 T.	lemon juice
1/3 c.	flour	1 c.	oatmeal
1/2 c.	brown sugar	1/2 t.	salt
1 t.	cinnamon	1/3 c.	butter, melted

Bake as above and serve with top milk or cream.

"We dried our own beef and apples. We cut the apples in rounds and strung them on strings like popcorn. They were hung over the wood cooking range to dry".

Ann Kramer
Eau Claire, WI

Yummy Apple Dessert

Another good recipe is this quickly made apple treat to be served warm or cold with plain whipped cream.

Mix: 1 c.   flour
           1/4 c. sugar

Cut in 1/3 c. butter or margarine. Pat into sq. baking tin. Bake at 350F for 20 min. Beat 2 eggs until thick; add 1 c. brown sugar and beat again. Add vanilla and 2 or 3 diced apples.

Sift: 1/2 c. flour
          1 t.   baking powder
          1/4 t. salt

Stir into apple mixture. Pour over crust and bake at 350F for 35 min.

A delicious, simple-to-prepare dessert is remembered by Ginny Solberg of Menomonie, WI, as made in the 1930's by her mother, Virginia Ray. It is called:

Marguarites

Beat 4 egg whites stiff but not dry. Gradually add 1-1/2 c. sugar* while beating until stiff peaks form. Add 1 t. vanilla. Fold in finely chopped walnut meats, about 1 c. Drop by spoonfuls on soda crackers. Bake in 300° oven till golden brown, or from 25-35 min.

*Only 1 c. of sugar may be used with good results.

Meringue Kisses

Beat 4 egg whites till stiff but not dry. Add 1/4 t. salt and 1 c. sugar gradually while beating 5 more min. Add 1 t. maraschino cherry juice, 3/4 c. chopped nuts. Grease pan lightly. Bake at 250F for 1 hr. Makes 4 doz.

When egg yolks were used for noodle-making, the egg whites were put to good use as these recipes show. Macaroons were a delicacy and when coconut was available, this old-fashioned recipe was used.

Old-Fashioned Macaroons

Start oven at 350F. Cover cooky sheets with waxed paper.
Beat: 2   egg whites
     1/8 t. salt
     1/8 t. cream of tartar till soft peaks form.
Add: 1 t. vanilla
Add: 3/4 c. sugar very gradually, beating until stiff
        peaks form
Fold in: 1-1/2 c. moist shredded coconut

Drop from tsp. onto waxed paper. Bake 25 to 30 min., or until golden and baked through. Some recipes call for baking longer.

To make corn flake macaroons, use 2 c. corn flackes and 1 c. coconut. Nuts may be added. For variation, grated orange peel is sometimes added.

Meringues ala Belle

Even children learned to make these treats whenever egg whites were left over.

Beat 3 egg whites till soft peaks form. Gradually add 3/4 c. sugar, beating until stiff peaks form (the kind that stand up). Blend in 1 t. vanilla, 1/2 t. baking powder. Fold in 1/2 c. crushed soda crackers, 1/2 c. nuts (optional). Drop on greased cooky sheet. Bake at 300F for 20 min., or till baked through. Remove from pan while still warm.

Some old recipes call for baking at a lower temperature for an hour. These produce a dry product and not as chewy as the above recipe.

Here is a cooky recipe we made and sold from house-to-house in Minneapolis in 1932 for 10-cents a dozen at first. When they sold very well we raised the price to 15-cents, but we also made them a little bigger.

Honey Cookies

2 c. brown sugar, 1 c. lard (or any shortening). Mix and add 1 beaten egg, 2 c. honey. Mix well. Dissolve 2 T. baking soda in 1 c. hot water. Add 2 t. ginger, 1 T. cinnamon, 1 T. salt, and flour enough to handle. Roll out, but and bake in 350™ oven 10 to 12 min.

I. Parker
Eau Claire WI

MY FAMILY HERITAGE OF RECOLLECTIONS AND

HAPPENINGS OF THE 1930s.

Date Recorded_____

MY FAMILY TREASURY OF HEIRLOOM RECIPES

Date Recorded_____

Through the leanest of the lean years, children learned that they had to help out and give up their gifts or earnings for the support of the family. One such happening took place at Urbank, Minnesota.

BUDDY BOUGHT THE FLOUR

As fall hunting season approached, my five-year-old brother Buddy was given instructions on how to open the big swinging farm gate. City hunters would soon arrive to drive through as they came to hunt on our family farm. Buddy was sent out with the anticipation that he would be rewarded with a few coins. He was barely tall enough to manipulate this masterful feat, but he did as he was taught and he did it well.

However, times were hard in the cities, too, and Buddy came back with only a few coins which he handed directly to my father. Having absolutely nothing in the house to prepare lunch with, and no money other than the few coins, my father hurried to the village for just enough flour so my mother could prepare a batch of good yeast buns before the hunters would return. People were always fed in those days, no matter what or how little appeared on the table. Everyone shared.

My mother was an expert bread baker and in no time at all her batch of crusty brown light and high buns were cooling on the table. About that time the hunters were observed coming from all directions heading for the farmstead on the pretext of asking my father where the birds were hiding. Of course they were invited in to eat. My mother fried a large pan of eggs and opened her last jar of dill pickles. Butter was on the table.

It seemed to us children that they ate for hours. We had not eaten and had to wait to see if there might be any left over.

As they finally got up from the table, thanking my parents for their hospitality, several more coins were given to a younger three-year-old brother who was standing there in awe of these rugged men with their big guns who ate so much and so long.

When my mother cleared the table, she found a quarter under one of the plates. The coins were all handed to my father who now had enough to buy a 98-cent sack of flour.

He was back quickly and my mother soon had another pan of bread started, using her usual potato-yeast starter. In no time it was raised high enough for the family to have pan-fried bread.

This was made from the first rise of the bread. Handfuls of soft dough was cut off, flattened and fried in the big, old cast iron pan, using pure lard. They raised in the hot frying grease, making air bubbles. My mother fried them crisp on the outside and tender and light on the inside. She sprinkled sugar on them as they came out of the pan. She fried a large serving platter of these and none were left over. I can't recall anything ever being left over.

Buddy's sister
Menomonie WI

Breads

How we got our flour

"During the 1930's every community had it's flour mill and we had Dobmeyers Roller Mill. Now most of these mills are no longer milling flour and it's by products which is what this is all about.

The farmers came with wagons and horses bringing a load of wheat or rye. The miller got his pay out of the wheat.

All was ground into white flour although often it contained much of the original kernel when the mill was in it's early stone grinding period.

The ground wheat was then passed through many siftings. First to remove the outer shell, which is bran. This was used for feed, mostly for the poultry. The second sifting produced middlings. This was used to bake graham bread as well as the muffins and pancakes. Muffins were known then as Gems. Grandma Joos baked them regularly and so did I by the time the hard times were upon us on the farm.

What was left of the flour consisted of crushed kernels and was used as a cereal for breakfast food. It required longer cooking so we learned to start it in the evening in our waterless cookers which we received as a premium when we subscribed for "The Farmer's" magazine. We enjoyed this cereal particularly with brown sugar and milk.

109

Along with this Mr. Dobmeyer created his own "Cream of Wheat" cereal. He became so efficient in this that it became the leading (most used) cereal and was sent even to St. Paul and Minneapolis. (Simply by using a variety of grains, corn and oats too). It was very delicious and certainly nutritious.

Mr. Dobmeyer was a first class engineer as he learned how to use his mill to produce all these various products. Not all millers did all this but all produced middlings and whole wheat flour. These products were the mainstay for our food along with the vegetables and what grew wild.

Every cook soon learned how to prepare these wheat products wholesomely. There was never any left for the dog so I took ground grain used as hog feed, mixed it with thick sour milk, fat drippings if we had any and baked it in the oven.

Yes, even salt was scarce. So much better for us. That was real salt, thick heavy kernels taken out of the wooden staved barrel. It needed sifting too so we used only the finer parts.

Our honey came from the hollow trees, very delicious too, pure and nutritious. Raisins sold for 5 cents a pound as did prunes, and dried apples. To find that nickel was the real problem".

As written by the writer's Mother at age 87
Helen J. Cichy
Millerville, MN

The Staff of Life

Bread and biscuits were staples every cook knew very well how to prepare. Batches of bread were large, consisting of eight loaves or more. The last loaf occasionally was used for cinnamon rolls. Children coming home from school came to expect fresh cinnamon rolls to be ready on bread baking day. Even so, they still had a big appetite for their dinner.

Lard was used in bread baking. Kneading the dough well was the secret to light, crusty delicious bread. It would bulge generously over the pans as it came out of the oven.

Some women learned to "rest" the dough ten minutes before

kneading which allowed time for the gluten to moisten and
for the dough to firm up. Eight or ten minutes of
kneading was needed to make the dough springy and elastic.
Bread was baked every few days. Farm lunches, school
lunch pails, and big breakfasts took many loaves daily.

The following method provided delicious white bread for
the family of H.J. Cichy of Minnesota.

Starter yeast was used for many years giving it a
distinctive yeast flavor. When dry yeast was affordable
and available it was used as in the recipe which follows.

White Bread Nutritious & Delicious

Dissolve:
2 pkg.   dry yeast — in
1/2 c.   warm water
1 t.   sugar

Sift:
16 c.   flour — into a generous size bowl. Push flour
to side of bowl to make a cavity in center.

Into another bowl:
1/2 c.   lard, soft or melted
2 T.   salt
1/2 c.   sugar
1 c.   hot water

Stir and blend till all is dissolved. Add: 5 c. cool
water. When this is luke warm add the yeast mixture.
Reserve 1/4 c. of the flour to add while kneading. Mix
well, kneading in the 1/4 c. of flour. Cover with a
cloth. Set in a warm place out of the draft. Allow to
rise till double in bulk. Knead down very well and allow
to rise again. Form into 8, 1b. loaves or 7 loaves and
rolls; recipe follows. Let rise again until all corners
of the pans are filled and the bread is nicely rounded.
Preheat oven to 350F. Place pans carefully in oven so
heat can circulate. Bake for 45 min. without opening the
oven door. Bread is done when tapping on top of the loaf
produces a hollow sound. Remove pans as soon as it comes
from the oven and cool on racks. Remember when preparing
the bread for the pans to grease them generously so the
bread slips out easily. Bread to be frozen must cool no
less than 12 hrs.

111

Cinnamon Rolls Made From Bread Dough

Use dough from 1 loaf of bread. Pat into a large square. Butter generously. Sprinkle with a mixture of 6 T. brown sugar and 1 t. cinnamon. Roll up like a jelly roll and cut into 1-1/2" pieces. Place into a pan prepare with a generous greasing of fat and brown or white sugar. Place rolls into pan and let rise till double in bulk. Bake in 350F oven, before bread goes in for 20 min. Top rack may be needed in oven to prevent bottom from burning. Remove from oven and place pan upside down on clean towel for a few minutes. Remove pan and let rolls cool before eating.

* * *

Good fresh bread was served with many toppings when butter was scarce or sometimes not available.

Christine Klatt of Menomonie remembers mixing soft butter with whipped cream to extend it. Women were very innovative.

Plain whipped cream on bread was a big favorite or simply thick cream ladled on with a large spoon. Syrups made out of berries, actually it was intended to be jelly but with the sugar supply very limited it became syrup. This was drizzled on the thick cream for a gourmet flavor.

It is well to keep in mind that cream has a lot less calories than butter and makes many an otherwise plain meal a very tasty one.

Corn syrup was probably the most popular bread topping because it was inexpensive and went a long way. Honey and sorghum were used also because they could either be found in the woods or grown in the fields.

Often the bread didn't come out of the oven fast enough, the last having been used for the previous meal or lunches. Women soon learned to make what became a great favorite, the Fried Bread.

Fried or Panned Bread

Whatever they called it, it was popular and well remembered by many and still made by some.

When everyone came in for lunch and the bread was rising nicely in the dough pan and far from being ready for the oven, the cook quickly got out the big cast iron fry pan.

To this she added a big spoonful of lard, cut off handfuls of the soft rising dough, patted it in flat rounds and fried it. When both sides were browned it was put on the platter and sprinkled with sugar.

It was a good lunch and kept everyone satisfied until the next meal.

Tasty Toast

When there was no butter available the ingenious cook would spread lard on bread and brown it lard side down in the fry pan. If syrup was plentyful it was drizzled on the crusty toast for added enjoyment.

Lard was also put on the table as is and spread like butter. Pan drippings from frying meat was considered especially good when heated in the fry pan and served in the heavy cast pan to keep it warm.

Eggs In a Circle

Was born out of the piece of toast above with a hole cut out of the center. One side was browned, turned, spread with lard and an egg dropped in the center and seasoned. The toast was turned once more to cook the egg on both sides. The center of the piece of toast was browned also for an extra morsel of goodness.

This lunch was generally made for a quick snack when nothing else could be found to eat. It was a delicious snack.

Florence's Yummy Buns

Pour: 1 c.   boiling water — over
           1/2 c.   shortening
           1/2 c.   sugar
           1-1/2 t. salt

Stir and cool to lukewarm; add 2 beaten eggs. Dissolve 2 cakes of yeast in 1 c. of warm water for 5 min. Add to above mixture. Add flour gradually beating well to a total of approximately 6 c. Lots of kneading gives a good texture.

Florence Gaffaney
Alexandria, MN

Mayme's Kolaches

The depression never got so bad that these delicious treats couldn't be made in the Bohemian areas, at least for the holidays.

2 c. scalded milk cooled to luke warm; add 1 cake of yeast and 2 T. of sugar out of 1/2 c. Add flour to make a soft sponge; let rise 1 hr. Add 1 beaten egg, rest of sugar, 4 T. melted lard and salt. Make a very soft dough; let raise 1-1/2 hrs. Makes 30. Add cinnamon and vanilla to prune filling.

Fillings

Prune filling:
Cook: 1 c.   prunes

Add: 1/2 c.   orange juice

Mix: 1 T.   flour with
          1/2 c.   sugar
          1/8 t.   salt

Cook until thick.

Add: 1/2 c.   nuts, chopped
         some   cinnamon
         some   vanilla

(Continued on next page)

114

(Continued from last page)

Apricot filling:
Cook: 1 lb.   apricots, dried

Add: 1/2 c.   orange juice
           1/2 c.   water

Mix: 1 c.   sugar
           2 T.   flour
           1/8 t.   salt
           1 t.   orange rind

Cook until thick.

Hot Cross Buns

This is an an Old Swedish recipe used through the
depression. There was little money for candy or even egg
color, they improvised it themselves, but Easter Sunday
many a family had a version of this special once a year
treat.

Combine: 1-1/2 c. milk, scalded
           1/2 c.   butter
           1/3 c.   sugar

Cool to luke warm and add 1 cake of yeast. Dissolved in
1/4 c. luke warm water.

Add: 1 t.   salt   ] Beat until
           2   eggs, well beaten   ] light and
           2 c.   flour   ] bubbly.

Add: 1 c.   raisins
           1/3 c.   citron, chopped
           1/2 t.   powdered cardamom
           2-1/2 c.   flour

Knead well, put in greased bowl and set in warm place to
rise. Knead once, let rise until double in size; form
into small rolls and let rise till light. Brush with
melted butter. Cut cross through top with sharp knife.
Bake 15 min. Brush with butter and sprinkle with sugar, Or
drizzle with thin powdered sugar icing.

* * *

"We took wheat up to Menomonie and had it ground. The shorts I used for bread and muffins. The first break of the wheat I cooked for cereal. Also, we got corn ground and made Johnny Cake and Corn Meal Mush. We used Karo syrup on it. I used sorghum as well as honey for baking. We also got 50 lbs. of cracked rice for our use."

Ellen Johnson
Elk Mound, WI

Super Whole Wheat Bread

Whole grain cereal were used extensively through the 1930's which explains part of the healthful diets people of that era lived on. This is a modern version.

6 c.   warm water
3 T.   yeast
1/2 c.   honey (brown sugar OK too)

Dissolve above and add: 2 c.   powdered milk
                             7-9 c.   whole wheat flour

Beat 100 strokes and rise for 1 hr. Fold down and add 2 T. salt and 1/2 c. oil and   whole wheat flour. Knead with white flour. Shape into 4 loaves in well greased pans. Bake at 350F for 1 hr. or until nicely browned.

Mother's German Christmas Kuchen

Scald 3/4 c. milk and stir in 1/2 c. sugar, 1-1/2 t. salt, 1/2 c. butter or margarine. Cool to lukewarm.

Add 2 pkgs. yeast to 1/2 c. warm water. Stir to dissolve and add to warm milk mixture. Add 1 beaten egg and beat till smooth. Stir in 4 c. unsifted flour (saving a little for final kneading) mixed with 1 c. candied fruit with citron and 1/2 c. soaked raisins. Knead until smooth and elastic. Let rise. Punch down vigorously and form into two 8"x8" (approx.) pans. Mix 4 t. sugar with 1 t. cinnamon. Sprinkle generously on top, punching in gently with finger tips. Let rise till double. Bake at 375° for 30 min.

Whole Wheat Bread II

Another good whole wheat bread recipe using some white flour and molasses. People of the 1930's didn't have a large variety of foods, but what they did have was power packed with nourishment. This one and the one on the preceding page were popular at that time.

Scald: 3/4 c. milk

Add: 4 T. sugar
3-1/2 t. salt
6 T. shortening
3/8 c. molasses

Let cool to luke warm. Combine yeast cakes in 1-1/2 c. warm water in very large bowl for mixing. Stir until dissolved. Add milk mixture. Combine 4-1/2 c. whole wheat flour and 2 c. sifted white flour; add half to liquid. Beat until smooth. Stir in rest of flour and knead. Cover with shortening and proceed like for white bread.

Yeast Corn Bread

Dissolve: 1 pkg. yeast — in
1/4 c. warm water

Scald: 2 c. milk

Pour over: 1/3 c. lard
1/3 c. sugar

Cool and add: 2 eggs, well beaten
1 t. salt
and yeast mixture

Mix well and add: 4 c. flour
1/2 c. cornmeal

Rise till double in bulk. Bake in two bread tins at 350F for 45 min.

Velma Fenske Collection
Menomonie, WI

117

Old Fashioned Brown Bread

3 T.	shortening
3 T.	sugar
1 c.	sour or buttermilk
1 t.	soda
1 c.	graham flour
1 c.	white flour
some	salt
1	egg

Mix and bake in well greased bread tin. Bake at 350F for 1 hr.

Dorothy Ganong
Eau Claire, WI

This bread is especially good with baked beans. We ate it a lot when we were short of bread.

Dorothy Ganong

Biscuits by the Dozen

These fluffy white creations were made several times a week to extend the bread and were a good filling food.

They were made out of sweet or sour milk or buttermilk. Mothers in town also turned these out using water and became very adept at it.

Lard was cheap, the biscuits were rich, light and very tasty. They were prepared in place of potatoes when that crop had dried out the summer before.

Served with corn syrup and pan drippings or with gravy and when available side pork or butter, they warmed many a hungry stomach at almost any time of the day.

I remember leaf lard and apples as a delicious spread for bread.

B. Heins
Waukesha WI

118

Baking Powder Biscuits

Sift: 2 c.   flour
           3 t.   baking powder
           1 t.   salt — into a mixing bowl.

Add: 1/4 c.   shortening — and blend with pastry blender or two knives.

Add: 2/3 c.   milk and mix quickly. Pat out on floured board. Knead and cut out with cooky cutter. Bake for 15 or 20 min. in 400F oven or till browned. Serve hot from the oven.

For pot pie crust, roll only 1/2" thick and press edges to casserole dish. Make a slit on top.

For drop biscuits add 1 c. milk and bake as usual. Grease all pans well.

Buttermilk Biscuits

Mix the same as above using:

2 c.   flour
1/2 t.   soda
2 t.   baking powder
1 t.   salt

Cut in 1/4 c. cold shortening and mix with 1 c. buttermilk, or sour milk.

Soda Biscuits

Some families prepared these daily to be made fresh and served for any meal or lunch hot from the oven.

Mix as for baking powder biscuits using 2 c. flour, 1/2 t. baking soda, 3/4 t. salt. Cut in 1/3 c. shortening. Add 3/4 c. buttermilk or sour milk. Bake at 350° for 12-15 min.

Gravy for Biscuits or Potatoes

Heat in fry pan: 1/4 c.   fat
                    4 T.   flour

Brown on slow heat until golden. Gradually stir in 2 c. cold milk or water and cook a few min. more. Season to taste.

Left over pork or pork sausage added for variation is excellent.

Fried hamburger, drained and added to the above gravy and served with any kind of potatoes, mashed, boiled or baked, makes a very good meal.

Fresh side pork probably made the best gravy using fat from the fried side pork. Large families relied on this meal for good tasty food.

                            Cy Lamb
                            Chippewa Falls, WI

Wyla Vasey recalls her first tuna sandwich. She was a little girl living with her family in Redfield, South Dakota and the year was 1930.

Mary B., the banker's daughter, formerly from Minneapolis, was having a birthday party. The word got around that tuna sandwiches would be served. No one in Redfield, South Dakota, ever had tuna. The anticipation created quite a sensation and, says Wyla, she's never tasted anything quite like it since.

THEY SOLVED THE PROBLEM OF CLOTHING

It's incredible how women made do and clothed their families warm and well in spite of using no cash to do so. A basic pattern generally was used for all garments. If matching thread had to be used for the buttons and button-holes, it was saved from the original garment and rolled on a spool to smooth it out.

Caring and sharing was a way of life learned and taught by example. Children grew up with concern for others and without hesitation, doing what they could to help alleviate or relieve another's suffering. Such was the state of the situation when —

ANGIE HAD NO CLOTHES.

Wyla Vasey and her friends, Mary and Betty, were very good friends of Angie Smith. Wyla had lots of cute clothes because her mother recycled every old worn-out garment that came her way. She carefully removed all buttons and tied them together when they matched, and saved them all in a box for future use.

But Angie was sad and downhearted because she had very little to wear, and winters in South Dakota got very cold.

Wyla remembers discussing this with Mary and Betty, and of course something had to be done. So they decided they all would go through their closets picking out what they could spare and choosing items Angie needed. They kept piling clothes into Angie's arms as they pulled them off the hangers. All of a sudden they noticed great big tears spilling down Angie's soft little cheeks.

Since we had only one dress we changed the lace collar and cuffs to make it appear we had more dresses.

R. Weix
Elmwood WI

Clothes came from wherever we could get them such as older rags that were big enough to get pieces from. Our undertaker in town used to bring us clothes that people would get rid of when people died. We made blankets and whatever we could out of material that was usable. We also raised a couple of pigs for our winter sausage. When we look back at these times we feel they were the best times of our lives because we had to work things out ourselves as a family and made our own amusement.

Mrs. E. Hart
Oak Creek WI

No one foresaw the impending ominous future in the late 1920's, but a very few were fortunate if their timing happend to be just right.

Leonard Lone of Augusta, Wisconsin, had worked hard and very long hours in the lumbering business, and had saved frugally. By 1928 he had $3,000 in the bank, a girl friend named Lillian and an urge to settle down.

He drew out all of his money and bought a 120-acre farm for $2,000 cash. Then he bought a new 1929 Model A Ford, the classiest one on the market with a rumble seat in the back, for $675. He made his decisions just in time, because soon after the Bank of Augusta closed. A neighbor had his savings all in there and after the fateful morning of April 14, 1929, he had only the 15-cents that was in his pocket.

On November 6, 1930, Leonard and Lillian were married on his birthday. They had money left over to buy furniture for the house, and he was fortunate again in that he found employment with Eau Claire County for 75-cents an hour, and worked there throughout the entire Depression.

Submitted by Lillian Lone
Augusta WI

Onion Kuchen

A favorite in Door County in years gone by, this recipe is still Number One is many homes:

Stew 1 to 2 qts onions in 1/4 c. shortening.
Spread sweet bread dough in 9"x13" pan.
Spread stewed onions over dough. Beat together and pour over onions: 2 eggs, 1 c. milk, 1/2 t. salt, 2 T. honey.
Sprinkle with bacon bits and caraway seed. Bake at 350™ about 45 min, after allowing time to rise.

S. Weix
Elmwood WI

Puddings

MY FAMILY TREASURY OF HEIRLOOM RECIPES

Date Recorded_____

Puddings

Cornstarch Puddings

They were also called Water Puddings, Vanilla Puddings and Delicious Puddings. The last one possibly named to prevent revealing the contents of this simple popular dessert. And of course, the Blueberry Fool.

Then there were the Vailings and the Sauces used as toppings, all made out of water with a bit of thickening and flavor. Vanilla or nutmeg were common flavors in the sauces and in the puddings. Butter was occasionally added and then it was called butter sauce. It was something to put on the table.

Like so many inexpensive recipes, this was another of the gallant efforts women made in their struggle to set an appealing meal before their men and to satisfy the ever hungry appetites of the children.

Everyone knew how to prepare these puddings and everyone did. Methods were as various as the contents of the pantries permitted.

Some households couldn't afford sugar so they sweetened the puddings and sauces with honey. Others added a bit of nutmeg to the cream poured over, or just any variation to keep the family in good spirits.

Gertie Bauer and her family never lost the taste for these yummy puddings. Her husband even today prepares it now and then made out of milk for "breakfast". That's not surprising.

In the 1960's cornstarch pudding was included in one of Jackie Kennedy's state dinner menus. Of course, it was called Blanc Mange and Mary Onstad of Menomonie, WI, has the recipe which follows on p. 131.

Cornstarch Pudding Basic Recipe

Bring 2 c. of water to a boil.

Mix:
4 T.	cornstarch
3 T.	sugar
3 T.	cold water

Mix with:
| 1/3 c. | cold water |

Slowly pour boiling water into it and boil 5 min. or until it is thickened. Remove from stove, add vanilla and salt. Pour into berry dishes rinsed in cold water. Serve with cream poured over.

Cream wasn't always available because it had to be sold for cash. Berries fresh or canned or fruit was added to the dishes to make a tasty dessert, as well as crushed nuts.

Variations included adding a square of chocolate or 3 T. of cocoa with a spoon of butter, the children's favorite, and a very elegant one adding the beaten whites of 2 eggs. It was returned to the stove to set the eggs and the juice of a lemon or lemon extract and a pinch of salt were added.

1931 Cornstarch Pudding using Milk

Scald:
| 1 c. | milk |

Mix:
2 T.	cornstarch
2 T.	sugar
2 T.	water
pinch	salt

Pour scalded milk slowly into mixture stirring constantly. Cook over hot water till thick and smooth; add flavoring. Pour into wet berry dishes. Chill and serve with cream or sauce made of berries or fruit.

Brown sugar was used to give it a caramel flavor and then came the snow pie. This one took a bit more sugar and 2 eggs and cream so it didn't often fit into many meal plans, but it was good.

Snow Pie

Mix: 3/4 c.   sugar (1/2 in some recipes)
        pinch   salt
        1 T.   cornstarch, heaping

Add: 1 c. cold water — and boil till clear

Beat: 2   egg whites — and fold into above mixture

Add: some vanilla — and pour into baked crust

Top with whipped cream, coconut, or fruit.

Puddings: —

Dorothy Waterman
Eau Claire, WI

Delores Papenfus
Mondovi, WI

Elsie Dallman
Chippewa Falls, WI

Hazel Ottman
Elmwood, WI

Grace Lacke
Augusta, WI

Lucille L.
Cadott, WI

And others.

Blueberry Fool

Wash 3 c. of blueberries and put in sauce pan. Add 3/4 c. sugar and bring to a boil. Dissolve 2 T. cornstarch in 1/2 c. water and bring to a boil again. 1 t. lemon juice may be added but is not necessary. Pour into berry dishes and serve warm or cold with cream.

This dessert was made with almost any kind of berry. A teaspoon of butter could be added but generally wasn't necessary either, especially when butter was scarce and had to be saved for bread, or there was none available at all.

Caramel Pudding

Or sometimes called "Burnt Sugar Pudding", had a distinctive caramelized sugar flavor.

Melt slowly: 1 c. sugar - in heavy pan until caramel color

Add: 1 c.   water, stir to dissolve

Add: 1 c.   milk and bring to slow boil

Mix: 2 T.   cornstarch in 1/2 c. water

Add to milk mixture and simmer till it thickens.

Mrs. Verner Hays
Eau Claire, WI

Velvet Pudding

Whenever flour was used to thicken these puddings they became smooth and velvety like this pudding named for it's texture.

Melt: 3 T.   butter

Add: 3 T.   flour — Stir well over low heat.

Add: 2 c.   milk — all at once stirring
                   continuously. Cook a few minutes.

Add: 1/4 c.   sugar
          pinch   salt
          some   cinnamon — to taste

Good as is or with cream.

Brown Sugar Cornstarch Pudding

Mix: 1 c. brown sugar (some recipes used 1/2 c. or 2 c.)
     4 T. cornstarch

Add: 1/2 c.   cold water

Add to: 1-1/2 c. boiling water

Cook till thick and smooth, while stirring; add vanilla and nuts. Serve in berry dishes with cream.

Brown Sugar Butter Sauce

Mix: 1/2 c.   brown sugar
           2 T.   cornstarch

Dissolve: in 1/2 c. cold water

Add to: 1/2 c. boiling water

Cook till syrupy, about 5 min. Add vanilla, butter and pinch of salt; cool.

Butter Sauce

Recipe same as above but uses white sugar.

Cottage Pudding

Ladle butter sauce over dry cake. Best served with warm sauce. Berries were added for further enjoyment.

Rhubarb Pudding

Another inexpensive pudding to "fill the cracks" was this simple dessert. Cook young rhubarb until tender. Sweeten to taste (or however much sugar you could spare) Thicken with a little cornstarch mixed with water. Cook 1 min. longer. Serve cold with cream.

Dorothy Waterman
Eau Claire, WI

Poor Man's Pudding

Combine: 1/3 c.   brown sugar] And
         1 c.   flour   ] spread
         1 t.   baking powder] in a
         pinch   salt   ] baking
         1/2 c.   milk   ] pan.

Mix: 1 c.   brown sugar] Pour over
         2 c.   hot water   ] batter and
         1 T.   butter   ] bake at 350F
         1/2 t.   nutmeg   ] for 1/2 hr.

Elsie Dallman
Chippewa Falls, WI

Old Fashioned Bread Pudding

Any time there were 6 slices of dry bread left over this delicious pudding was made. Less sugar was used when it was scarce which was always, and it was still very tasty. Butter also was omitted at times. Generally, good rich milk was used.

In buttered casserole arrange 6 slices of dry bread, sprinkling 1/2 c. raisins between slices.

Beat: 1/2 c.   sugar
            4 eggs, slightly

Add: 1/4 t.   ginger
            1 T.   butter, melted
            4 C.   milk, scalded

Pour over bread and let stand for 20 min. Bake at 325F covered for 30 min. Uncover and bake till nicely browned. Serve warm with cream.

Another recipe calls for 1/3 c. sugar and vanilla flavor.

Or 2 eggs, 1/4 c. sugar, 1/2 c. raisins, 1/2 t. cinnamon, 1 t. lemon extract, 6 slices of bread and 1 qt. of milk. Same method.

Or same as above, add butter to bread before cutting into cubes. Bake in blue roaster 40-45 min.

V.F.   Collection

Creamy Rice Pudding

Rinse well:
1/2 c.   rice — and put in baking dish or double boiler.

Add: 1 qt.   milk] Cook, stirring occasionally,
            3 T.   sugar] for 1 hr. or until rice can
            1/4 t.   salt] be seen from the top.

Add: 1 t.   vanilla
            1/2 c.   raisins, washed
            1   egg, beaten, last 30 min.

Serves 6.

Flummery

Cook until soft: 2 c. blackberries or any berries, with
                       2 c. water

Mix: 1 c.   sugar
        4 T.   cornstarch
        1/4 t.   salt

Add to above mixture and cook 5 min.; add 1 t. lemon
extract or juice. Pour into berry dishes and serve with
cream.

1938 Butterscotch Pudding

Mix: 3/4 c.   brown sugar
        3 T.   flour

Add: 1   egg   1/4 t.   salt
        1 T.   butter   3 T.   water

Mix and Add: 1 c.   milk

Bring to boil and boil until smooth and satiny; add
vanilla. Pour into pudding dishes and serve with cream.

For pie double the recipe and save white of eggs for
meringue. Beat stiff and add 1/3 c. sugar very gradually
until stiff peaks form; add vanilla. Bake till light
brown.

Mildred B.
Millerville, MN

Blanc Mange
(as served at the White House state dinner)

Mix 2 T.   cornstarch
    1/3 c. sugar
    1/8 t. salt
Combine with 1/2 c. milk and add to 1-1/2 c. scalded milk
in double boiler. Cook and stir until thick. Cover and
cook 15 min. longer. Add vanilla. Pour into sherbets
rinsed with cold water. Chill until firm. Dollup of whipped cream may be added. For a more delicate pudding, fold
two beaten egg whites in.

Apple Dumpling Pudding

Heat applesauce in heavy pan. If too thick add a bit of water.

Make dumpling as follows:-

2 c.	flour
1/2 t.	salt
4 t.	baking powder
1	egg, well beaten
3 T.	butter
2/3 c.	milk, or enough to make a moist stiff batter.

Drop dumplings in applesauce. Cover very closely, cook for 12 min. Do not lift cover. Serve hot with fresh cream, and sauce ladled over.

The above was actually a supper meal to fill out an otherwise not so ample table.

Helen C.

Berry, Peach or Apples Dumplings

When the imagination was depleted and there were some berries or fruit of any kind to be had, the following dish was put together and always was a winner.

Make a pastry as for pie. Roll out and cut into squares. In a baking pan, bring to a boil 1 c. brown sugar and 1 c. water.

Fill squares with fruit and a bit of sugar. Fold edges together. Place in pan side by side. Bake about 40 min. or until the crust is golden. Bast with the juice 4 or 5 times. If fruit is sour use more brown sugar.

Serve hot or cold with cream or with the juice only.

Virginia Ray of Menomonie, Wisconsin, remembers making a very tasty dessert using stale doughnuts slit in two. A white sugar butter sauce (see p. 129) was poured over while hot. Sometimes nutmeg was added. And for company, it looked elegent in stemmed sherbets.

Ozark Pudding

This apple pudding was a real winner. Topped with whipped cream or plain cream it was the grande finale to many a plain meal.

Beat:
2   eggs
1 c.   sugar — till very smooth.

Mix:
2 T.   flour   ] Add to
1-1/4 t.   baking powder] egg mixture.
1/8 t.   salt   ]

Add:
1/2 c.   nuts (optional)   ] Bake in greased
1 c.   apples, coarsely chopped] pie tin at 350F
1 t.   vanilla   ] for 35 min.

Rhubarb Tapioca Pudding

Cook:
3 c.   rhubarb, cut up
4-1/2 T.   quick tapioca
1/8 t.   salt
1-1/8 c.   sugar
2 c.   water

Stir while cooking. Cool and add 1-1/2 c. strawberries Top with whipped cream or plain cream.

Raisin Pudding

This recipe is over 50 years old and is still popular in this family.

Stir together:
1 c.   flour   ]
1/2 c.   sugar   ] Pour into
2 t.   baking powder] greased
1 c.   raisins   ] baking pan.
1/2 c.   milk   ]

Stir together:
1 c.   brown sugar
1 T.   butter
2 c.   boiling water

Pour over batter, bake at 350F until it's brown. Serve with cream, ice cream, warm or cold.

Lucille Schmidt—Cadott, WI

No doubt one of the very best of the old-fashioned bread puddings is this:

French Bread Pudding

Cube 6-8 slices of stale bread. Pour over about 1/2 c. salted water. Mix well by hand and press to dry and drain.

Beat:	2 eggs well
Add:	1/4 c. sugar
	1/2 c. seeded raisins
	and the bread
Scald:	1 qt. milk
Add:	1/2 t. cinnamon
	1 t. lemon extract

Pour over bread and stir well. Place into 2 qt. casserole baking dish and place in pan of hot water. Bake at 250-350° for 45-60 min. Serve hot, warm or cold. Serve with light cream or a dollup of Cool Whip. Only 90 calories witnout the light cream. Cool Whip is 12 calories per tablespoon. 1 serving is 1/16th of the entire.

Dolores Stensrud
Brandon MN

Burnt sugar cakes and puddings became popular through the Great Depression because they offered variety while using the same basic ingredients. Mrs. Vernon Hays of Eau Claire WI shares her delicious recipe called:

Caramel Pudding

Melt 1/2 c. sugar slowly over slow heat until it turns a caramel color. Add 1 c. water. It will sputter and some will harden, but will melt again. Add 1 c. milk and heat to slow boil. Add 2 T. cornstarch dissolved in water and cook until thickened. Serve warm or cold, with or without cream.

Muffins

Frugality in the kitchen was not a sole characteristic of women. Men came up with some very ingenious tricks of their own when the occasion called for it. The following testimonial comes from Manitowish Waters WI.

I worked as a meat department manager from 1928 to 1972 at the Hillmans Pure Foods, one of the largest in Chicago at that time. For thirty-five years I worked as a fireman and a fireman cook. In one of my recipes I used chicken feet. The nails would be cut off and the feet scalded to remove the skin. This would make the best soup with no fat. Also, to make clam chowder, Boston- or New England-style, we would take calf or beef brains, put them in salt water to remove the membrane, and cut them fine to the size of clams. You would never know the difference. My mother would use flour and sugar sacks from the baker to make dresses and shirts.

William P. Burger
Manitowish Waters WI

Muffins

Friendship Recipe

Take 4 parts genuine interest in other fellow. Strain to
remove any bits of curiosity. Add what tastes in common
you have and pleasant conversation as it seems to be
needed. Stir at unexpected intervals with a kind act and
cook until rich and smooth.

This will keep indefinitely, but should not be stored
away. Keep it handy and use daily.

* * *

Thanks

Thank God for dirty dishes
    They have a tale to tell
While others may go hungry
    We're eating very well

With home, health and happiness
    I shouldn't want to fuss
By the stack of evidence
    God's been good to us.

Muffins with Variations

These morsels are excellent just plain but a cook with ingenuity can add a lot of delicious surprises to them.

Sift together: 1 c.   flour
                1-1/2 t. baking powder
                1/2 t.   salt
                1-1/2 T. sugar

Melt: 1-1/2 T. butter

Add: 1 c.   milk
        1   egg, well beaten

Mix and add to flour mixture. Mix only to moisten. Grease muffin tins well. Preheat oven to 425F; bake for 25 min.

For Variations:

Add: t. jelly in center before baking.

Mix: Chopped dates, raisins, nuts or apricots in flour.

Add: Chopped crisp bacon to batter.

Add: 1/4 t. each of ginger, cinnamon, allspice and cloves to flour.

Add: Any kind of berry.

Make Sally Lunn by using 2 eggs, saving whites to beat stiff and fold in.

Fluffy Cornmeal Muffins

These were favorites with the Johnny Cake crowd and were made either with sugar or without.

When made without sugar they were used as a meal with syrup and bacon or fried pork.

When sugar was added they were served with butter as part of a meal or a lunch.

Sift together:

1 c.	cornmeal
1-1/2 c.	sifted flour
2 t.	baking powder
1 t.	soda
1-1/2 t.	salt
3 t.	sugar

Beat: 1 egg, until thick

Add:

1 c.	sour milk or buttermilk
4 T.	butter, melted

Combine and stir only to moisten. Bake in muffin tins 2/3 full for 20 min. at 425F. Serve hot.

Berry Muffins

Wash and dry: 1 c. wild or any berry

Sift into bowl:

3 c.	flour
1/2 c.	sugar
1 T.	baking powder
1 t.	salt

Add:

1/2 c.	milk
1/2 c.	butter, melted
3	eggs, slightly beaten

Blend and add berries. Fill muffin pans 2/3 full. Bake for 20 min. at 400F or till nicely browned.

Serve fresh and hot for breakfast or for light evening meal accompaniment.

Cream Puffs

Add: 1/4 c.   butter — to   ] Heat until butter
        1/2 c.   water   ] is melted.

Add:-   1/2 c. sifted flour all at once. Beat over heat
until smooth ball forms. Cool slightly and add 2 eggs,
not beaten, and stir in same direction, mixing well. Drop
on cookie sheet from a T. Bake at 350F for 1 hr. or more.
Puffs should be dry in cracks when done. Serve with
whipped cream filling.

These puffs were economical and quick to make, and
everyone liked them.

Today we also make them smaller and use for teas and
luncheons with fillings, as well as for desserts with
whipped cream and or a pudding blended in.

Ham, tuna or egg sandwich filling makes these a gourmet
luncheon plate.

Funnel Cakes

This treat was made by the Dutch on Sunday afternoons.
They were eaten hot and fresh and were popular in the
1930's because they didn't take much sugar to make.

Beat: 1   egg

Add: 2/3 c.   milk

Sift: 1-1/3 c.   flour

Add: 2 T.   sugar
        1/4 t.   salt
        1 t.   soda
        3/4 t.   baking powder

Add:- to milk and egg mixture. Fry in hot fat at 375F
using funnel with 5/8" opening. Holding finger over
funnel bottom measure 1/4 c. batter at a time. Swirl in a
circle as batter runs from funnel. These are good dusted
with powdered sugar.

Apple Muffins

Mix: 2 c.   flour
             4 t.   baking powder
             1-1/2 T. sugar
             1 T.   brown sugar
             1/2 t.   salt
             1/4 t.   cinnamon

Mix together: 1   egg, beaten
                   2 T.   butter, melted
                   1 c.   milk

Stir into flour. Fold in 1 c. diced, peeled apples and a few nuts. Pour into greased muffin tins; sprinkle with sugar and cinnamon. Bake for 20 min. in 400F oven.

Apple Muffins

Another recipe calls for the following variation.

Beat: 1   egg

Add: 1/2 c. milk   1/4 c. oil
           1-1/2 c. flour   1/2 c. sugar
           2 t.   baking powder   1/2 t. salt
           1/2 t. cinnamon

Fold in 1 c. unpeeled apples. Bake as above.

Graham Muffins Or Gems

Sift: 1 c.   white flour
          1 c.   graham flour
          2-4 T. sugar OR 1/4 c. honey
          1/4 t.   salt
          4 T.   baking powder

Beat: 2 eggs, well   Add: 3 T. fat, melted
                                  1 c. milk

Add:- to dry mixture and mix well. Bake in well greased muffin tins 20 to 25 min.

Honey was used in place of sugar in almost all dishes when sugar was in short supply. Honey has a unique flavor which adds to these gems.

Indian Corn Pone

Stir up for lunch before bread comes out of oven.

Combine: 1 c.   cornmeal
                1/2 t. salt
                1 t.   baking powder

Add: 2 T.   oil
                1/2 c. milk

Grease heavy skillet well. Drop batter into 4 pones. Brown on both sides.

Tasty Carrot Bread

This recipe is from a later date but is included for it's economical wholesome goodness.

Beat: 1 c.   sugar
       1/4 c. oil
       2   eggs

Add sifted together: 1-1/2 c. flour
                      1 t.   baking powder
                      1 t.   soda
                      1/4 t. salt
                      1 t.   cinnamon

Add 1 c. grated carrots and 1/2 c. nuts. Bake 1 hr. at 375F.

Rachel P.
Minneapolis, MN

NOTES:

Soups

I remember we ate a lot of potato soup and potato pancakes. The potato soup sometimes was made with water, and dried mushrooms were used to give it more body. Another food that stretched our menu was "cracklings." This was the leftover fat after lard was rendered. They were slightly salted and put into a container for future use. These would then be put in the oven to heat thoroughly and would be served with rye bread or boiled potatoes. The cracklings would sometimes be mixed with flour and baked on a cookie sheet to be eaten as a bread substitute.

Marie Larson
Rice Lake WI

Soups

Soup in the 1930's

"On Water Street in Eau Claire, Wisconsin, was a place called the Brown Derby where they served chicken. They precooked the chicken upstairs and if you climbed the outside stairs at the right time, you could buy the broth the chicken was cooked in. The cost was 5 cents a quart and you brought your own container.

At home noodles were being rolled out. If the quantity called for two eggs and you had only one the extra could be substituted with one egg shell full of water. This made a good filling meal."

Mrs. Douglas Whinnery
Eau Claire, WI

The neighbor was not so fortunate. A nickel was hard to come by. So the broth had no meat juice or bone in it. A spoon of lard added to seasoned water was the base for her soup.

Old Fashioned Vegetable Soup

Have on hand for quick lunches or suppers or for diets calling for one soup meal a day.

Cut meat off one soup bone and brown in heavy sauce pan. Add bone and 6 c. water.

Add:
1 c.	carrots, grated
1 c.	celery with leaves, cut up
2 c.	tomatoes
some	parsley, cut up
1 T.	salt
1/2	bay leaf
3	peppercorns
1/4 t.	marjoram
1/4 t.	thyme

A handful of any kind of noodles. Cook till done, 1 hr. or more. Can be frozen in serving size for quick warm up.

Cream Soups with Vegetables

These soups provide a lot of nutrition and can be used in a diet menu for lunch. A large bowl contains approximately 350 calories.

They are made out of every conceivable vegetable and are easy to prepare. Vegetable pulp can be made a day ahead and stored in the refrigerator for preparing a speedy meal.

They can be prepared with the dumplings for extra body or they can be creamed for a lighter meal and served with crackers.

Vegetable Soup

Cook vegetables until tender in water to barely cover. Puree in blender with the juice.

Use 2 c. in large heavy pan; add 3 c. milk. Season with salt, pepper and savory salt. Bring to gentle boil and add dumplings or thicken with butter and flour.

* * *

Dumplings

1/2 c.   flour   **OR for med. stiff batter**
1/2 t.   baking powder
some   salt

Mix well; add 1 egg and mix well again. Drop from spoon, cutting pieces size of an almond with butter knife dipped in soup. Simmer 5 min. uncovered, then simmer covered 5 min or more. Serve in large shallow bowl with pat of diet margarine in center and fresh black pepper for garnish.

Combinations of these good cream soups are as varied as the imagination. A real winner is the diced potato soup combined with a can of peas pureed, 2 c. of milk and 3 slices of bacon diced, fried and added without the grease.

146

Vegetable Suggestions:-

Broccoli	Sauté 1/2 onion and add to blender 1/2 c. grated mild cheese is optional
Cauliflower	1/2 c. sauté onion
Potato	Sauté 1/2 onion add to blender 1/2 c. mild cheese optional
Onion	
Canned Peas	Use as is and blend
Fresh Corn	Do not blend; sauté onion
Spinach	Blend, sauté onion
Potato diced	Sauté onion; do not blend
	1/4 c. parsley; Best prepared with dumplings

Thickening to use without dumplings: 2 T. flour mixed well with 2 T. butter or diet margarine. Pour soup into mixture and mix. Return to pan and boil several min.

Elegant Fish Soup

Almost any kind of fish fillets can be used for this great tasting soup. Commonly used were pan fish because the lakes were full of them.

Cook:
2 c.   fish fillets - several min. or until fish turns white. With a slotted spoon transfer to a large plate to cool.
Brown 2 strips of bacon cut up fine; pour off grease leaving enough to sauté 1/2 onion; add to broth. Add 3 diced potatoes, 1/4 c. fresh parsley and cook until potatoes are tender. Cut fish into small pieces and add to the soup. Season with seasoning salt, salt and pepper; add 3 c. milk. Mix 3 T. butter and 2 T. flour; add to soup and boil gently several min. OR add 1/3 c. potato flakes for thickening. Serve with a pat of butter and crackers. OR, as Eleanor Ostman stated in her Tested Recipes column in the St. Paul Pioneer Press, add allspice for a touch of variety.

147

Potato Onion Soup with Dumplings

Each time you boil potatoes, save the potato water.
(Nutritionists say that much of the food value is in the
potato water). Cook chopped onions in the potato water;
add a few potatoes mashed smooth. This soup base will
keep in the refrigerator up to five days. When ready to
use add some milk and seasonings, bring to a boil and drop
dumpling batter in it. No thickening is needed. It is a
delicious tummy filling food.

Doris Cronk
Menomonie, WI

Farina Dumplings

Bring to a boil:
1 c.	milk
1 t.	sugar
1/4 t.	salt
1 t.	butter

Add: 1/4 c. farina

Stirring constantly, cook till farina doesn't adhere to
sides of pan. Add 1 egg and beat well; drop from t. into
boiling clear soup. Chopped parsley may be added for
color and flavor. Cook 15 min. covered.

Lila B.
Germany

Bean Soup with Ham

Wash 2 c. dry navy beans and bring to a boil in 2 qts. of
water. Turn off and let stand for 1 hr. Add a meaty ham
bone or hocks; add no salt, only pepper. Add 1 lg. onion
cut up, 1 lg. carrot grated and celery seed or leaves.
Cook till all is done and beans are tender.

Sometimes a cup of cream was added before serving.

All I remember of those years is that we had bean soup too often.

Dolores Stensrud
Millerville, MN

"I remember too we ate a lot of potato soup and pancakes".

Marie Larson
Rice Lake, WI

Old Fashioned Potato Soup

Boil 8 potatoes until soft (diced), using as little water as possible. Beat lightly with beater leaving some chunky pieces; add 1 qt. milk, and seasoning.

Mix:
3 T.	flour or enough to make a drop batter
1 t.	baking powder
pinch	salt — and mix.

Add 1 egg and mix well. Drop by t. half full using butter knife dipped in milk soup. Cook 10 min. more covered tightly and turned on simmer.

Old Fashioned Tomato Soup

Fresh, canned or frozen tomatoes used in this recipe produces a light delicious soup anyone can be proud to serve. Care must be taken in combining the milk with the acid tomatoes to keep it from curdling.

Heat a qt. of tomatoes (pour some liquid off)
Add:	1/2 t.	soda
Heat:	2 c.	milk
Add:	salt, pepper and butter	

Pour hot tomatoes slowly into hot milk and serve with soda crackers.

Eva Mae W.
Menomonie, WI

Grot or Mehl Zuppe

The name depends on your nationality. The Scandinavians made Grot while the Germans made Mehl Zuppe. The only difference was that the Scandinavians elaborated. They also made the Romme Grot which was a rich version of the same. It was made out of cream and was buttery, with most of the butter having been skimmed off through the cooking process. The Grot made for an evening meal was made out of rich whole milk, like the German Zuppe.

Many a meal consisted of large wide bowls of Grot or Mehl Zuppe. Some liked it plain while others sprinkled it with sugar and cinnamon. There were generally so many around the table that each was served one large bowl. If that didn't satisfy them they filled up on bread, some kind of topping and coffee.

True Grot lovers and Mehl Zuppe eaters never get tired of this dish and even long for it today.

Grot or Mehl Zuppe

Heat to boiling: 1 qt. of milk in heavy sauce pan.
Mix: a heaping 1/2 c. of flour with cold milk till smooth. Dilute with hot milk and return to sauce pan. Add pinch of salt and boil gently for at least 10 min. Cooking brings out the true flavor of this dish.

To make Romme Grot one used cream. Half and Half may be used with good results.

Norwegian Dumplings

Bring to a boil:
1 c.	water	
1 T.	butter (heaping)	
pinch	salt	
1/2 t.	nutmeg	

Add: 1 c. flour — all at once

Stir till well mixed. Remove from heat. Add 3 eggs, one at a time, beating well after each addition or until batter is smooth. Drop by t. into hot soup at slow boil. Cook 10 min. with cover on.

Pickles

Grandpa was a carpenter and Grandma used the cement bags for towels. They were much stiffer and coarser than flour sacks, but eventually softened up a little. I still have one. The most anyone had going for themselves was the fact that it was something everyone had to live with, nobody had much. No one used supplemental "food stamps" to pick up groceries in a car. People were so ashamed that they postponed asking for help as long as possible. And you couldn't own a car and receive help. But cars didn't sell, so they often were sold in pieces — battery, tires, etc. I loved the simple foods —dumplings, made small and served with buttered bread crumbs. I though everyone ate dandelion green made with German hot dressing. Speaking of bacon, it has such a bad reputation that I was pleased to read recently of its dripping only having one third the cholesterol of butter.

Joan Gesbeck
Kenosha WI

We had a large family and used to buy 30 bushel of potatoes and we always had potatoes and gravy. We didn't have much meat, but what we did have was lots of gravy. And we had all the milk we could drink. In our family we had to be 14 years old before we could drink anything but milk. And then, after 14 we got "fairy tea." It was mostly milk with a little dab of tea.

Vivian Olson
Eau Claire WI

Pickles

Really Good Dills

Pack small washed cucumbers into sterile jars, starting with one grape leaf in bottom, and 1 clove garlic (optional).

Boil:
- 1 qt. vinegar
- 2 qts. water
- 1/2 c. salt (canning)
- 1 t. sugar (in each jar)

Pour over cucumbers; add dill. Seal and process 10 min.

Polish Dills

Pack small cucumbers into jar.

Add:
- 1 grape leaf
- 1 head dill
- 1 clove garlic

Boil:
- 1 qt. water
- 1 c. vinegar
- 3 T. canning salt (level)
- 1 T. sugar
- 1/8 t. tumeric
- some alum (size of a pea)

Boil 15 min. Pour over cucumbers. Seal and process 10 min.

Green Tomato Relish

2 gal. green tomatoes	6 red peppers
6 green peppers	10 med. onions
1 sm. head cabbage	1 t. celery seed
1/2 c. salt	8 c. vinegar
8 c. sugar	

Chop vegetables; add salt and let stand overnight. Drain; add vinegar, sugar and spices. Cook until vegetables are all cooked, about 30 min. Pack in hot sterile jars and seal.

Beet Horseradish Relish

1 qt.	beets, cooked and ground
1 qt.	cabbage, ground
1/2 c.	horseradish
2 c.	vinegar
3/4 c.	sugar
2 t.	salt

Bring to a boil. Pack into sterile pt. jars and seal. Process 20 min. Store.

Corn Relish

Cut corn from 18 cobs.

2	green peppers, chop or grind
2	red peppers, chop or grind
1 sm.	head of cabbage, chopped
4	onions
1 c.	celery, chopped

Add:

1 qt.	vinegar
2 c.	brown sugar
2 T.	salt
3 T.	mustard

Bring to a boil and cook until corn is tender, about 20 min. or so. Pack in sterile jars and seal. Makes 5 pts.

Extra Good Beet Pickles

Because the brine is mild, this is more than just a beet pickle and is enjoyed as a spiced beet vegetable.

Bring to a boil: 1 pt. beet juice
1 c. sugar
1 c. vinegar

Pour over sliced beets packed in sterile qt. jars to which has been added 1 t. pickling spice and 1" stick cinnamon. Seal and process 10 min.

Helen Joos Cichy
Millerville, MN

154

Stone Jar Cucumber Pickles

These pickles are extra special for flavor and they keep forever - the saying goes, but of course they never last long enough to really find out.

Wash and pack into a stone jar (crock):
1 bshl. med. size cucumbers

Bring to a boil, water and salt to float an egg. Pour over and let stand 24 hrs. Drain and wipe them dry. Cut in chunks or leave whole. Measure the salt and water and mix the same amount of water and vinegar and add to pickles. Let stand overnight. Drain again, and bring to a boil fresh water with equal part of vinegar and -

Add:
1 c.	dark brown sugar
2 c.	mustard seed
1 sm.	handful of whole cloves
1	handful of cinnamon sticks
some	alum (size of pullet egg)
1	handful of celery seed

Bring to a boil. Pour over cucumbers in crock after lining crock with 15 fresh grape leaves. Wet them and they will stick to the sides. Cover with a plate and rock. Will keep as is almost indefinitely and is good in a week or two.

From the collection of the late: Velma Lillian Fenske
Menomonie, WI

SEARCHING

Hundreds of thousands of young men roamed the country on trains in search of something, anything — food, an hour of work, a purpose to live — and they couldn't go home. There wasn't enough to eat. These young men went through very rough times. The real hoboes didn't turn them away, but gave them a tin can full of whatever they cooked up. The young men donated to the hoboes pot anything they could find or buy for a penny or a treasured nickel. It was food for an empty stomach.

In the 1937 Great Depression years, there still was no work. I decided to go to my Uncle George's place in North Dakota to see if there was work to be had. He was in the business of buying scrap iron and buffalo and cattle bones. I helped him for my room and board for awhile, but he had a family to provide for and, feeling I was a burden on him, I decided to go further west to try for work.

I boarded a Great Northern freight train in Minot, North Dakota, heading west. The railroads frowned on young men riding the freight cars, but during the Great Depression the government ordered the railroads to allow men to ride, mainly to keep unemployed young men moving so they wouldn't congregate in one place.

There were 15 of us riding in this Great Northern boxcar. It was getting late in the evening and we were well into Montana. It was late spring — March or April, I think — and it was getting cold. We had the sliding door on one side of the boxcar closed while the sliding door on the other side was open about a foot. All at once the train gave a jerk and the open door slammed shut, locking us inside the boxcar.

We all got up and tried to pry the door open, but try as we could, we couldn't get the door open. The other one was locked shut as well. It was very dark and we couldn't really see what we were doing. One man had a flashlight, but the batteries were low so we had little or no light at all. I was scared and so was everyone else. We thought there was a possibility the boxcar would be left on a siding somewhere in the middle of nowhere and we didn't know if we'd ever get out.

Some of us started to panic. One man had claustrophobia and started running around yelling, "Get us out! Get us out!" Nothing can describe the panic. I was afraid it would turn into a madhouse if it wasn't stopped. I grabbed him and hit him in the jaw as hard as I could and knocked him unconscious.

I knew we had to do something to get us out. I wore a pair of heavy work shoes with metal cleats on the heels. I took these off and gave one shoe to one guy and the other to another fellow and told them to pound on both doors until they were too tired and then to give the shoes to the next two pounding continuously in the hope of someone hearing us.

All this time the freight was moving. It seemed like hours until the freight started slowing down and finally stopped. We were still pounding on the doors more vigorously than before. We finally heard footsteps on the gravel outside the boxcar and then a brakeman opened the door. We were so relieved we yelled and cheered and couldn't get out of the boxcar fast enough. I almost jumped out without my shoes on, when I realized we'd been using them on the doors.

My travels continued. I traveled through Utah, Washington, Oregon and California only finding temporary jobs.

One of the jobs was painting the beams on a toll bridge over the Columbia River. This was scary because it was 63 feet above the water and to have fallen was sure death. I worked on a 12-inch-wide plank. That's why the job was available. Not many people were willing to risk it. I worked there two days and that was enough for me.

When I ran out of what little earnings I did make from time to time, desperate for food, I'd go up to a house and ask for something to eat. People were polite and offered me what they could. Sometimes I was turned down and other times they found work for me to do to earn my meal.

Finally, when no work was available anywhere, I returned to Minnesota and got a job for $3.00 a week, room and board included, working 16 hours a day in a village general store in Forada, Minnesota.

as told by George W. Van Amber
Menomonie WI

to Anita Van Amber
Green Bay WI

Brass beds were common. They were left over from the good times during and after World War I when prices were high and people had money. Everyone owned one or several brass beds and they kept them clean and shiny by cleaning with a mixture of 2 T. salt to 1 c. vinegar. This was mixed with flour and enough water to make a paste. It was brushed on and after 10 minutes or so it was washed off with warm soapy water and then rinsed well. It was polished with old wool cloths to a high sheen. This was done every spring at housecleaning time.

P. Johnson

In 1932 President Roosevelt was treated at the Mayo Clinic in Rochester MN. He was so impressed with the growing hospital and the excellent care he received that he presented the hospital with 13 solid gold plates of the disciples. These were later donated to the Smithsonian Institute.

Miscellaneous

Chemical Gardens – Home Rendered Lard

Wine and Beer

Etc.

Hash! Of course. Everyone knows about leftover beef (or any meat), potatoes, gravy, onions. I can still see my mother using a wooden bowl and chopper, mixing these leftovers for the fry pan. My husband used to enjoy creamed corn over hash.

Cecil Johnston
Milwaukee WI

As a kid I just didn't realize the hardships my parents went through to feed a family of five. I do remember the food tasting better then. Home grown vegetables, huge blueberries my folks picked west of Ashland by the tubsful which my mother canned in two-quart jars along with other canned fruits and vegetables. Fresh chickens -- fresh everything.

B. Amich
Ashland WI

Some of my memories are most vivid yet. I recall hunting the house over for 25-cents.

M. Hetzel
Milwaukee WI

I still like bean sandwiches. It's something I never did get tired of.

R.B. Stock
Brookfield WI

160

Miscellaneous

Chemical Garden

This was a centerpiece made out of coal, which was plentiful, and canning salt. It had it's origin through the drought when water became so scarce it couldn't be used for watering flowers.

Into a nice large glass bowl put 2 or 3 pieces of good sized coal. Pour 2 T. each of water, bluing and salt over it. Let stand a day and then add 2 more T. salt and water; add 3 drops of mercurochrome on each lump.

It will form interesting growth formations both attractive and colorful.

* * *

"We brushed out teeth with salt and soda".

Mrs. H.W.
Eau Claire, WI

Ginger Tea

"Our neighbor, who was also a midwife at the birth of several of the younger children, would come over carrying a bucket and a lard pail to tie around her waist and a jug of "ginger tea".

Mom and I and whichever of the others old enough to get through the briars got out straw hats and buckets and we'd go to the woods to pick blackberries, wild raspberries or dew berries in season.

When the wild blueberries were ripe she would send us out on our own, although she liked to be in the woods too. Also, wild strawberries because she didn't worry about our getting lost in the fields.

The ginger tea was made out of ground ginger, sugar and boiling water. Probably proportions to ones taste.

Mother had a lot of ways to make a little go a long way."

Julie W.
Mondovi, WI

161

How to Preserve a Husband

Be careful in your selection, do not choose too young. When once selected, give your entire thought to preparation for domestic use.

Some insist upon keeping them in a pickle, others are constantly getting them into hot water. This may make them sour, hard, and sometimes bitter; even poor varieties may be made sweet, tender and good.

Garnish them with patience, well sweetened with love and seasoned with kisses. Wrap them in a mantle of charity, keep warm with a steady fire of domestic devotion and serve with peaches and cream.

Thus prepared they will keep for years.

Most girls used this recipe in the 1930's and have stated that their husbands still show no signs of spoilage.

Dandelion Wine

Put 1 gal. flower heads into crock or enamel vessel. Pour over 3 qts. boiling water. After 7 days strain and wring out, then return to crock. Boil 1-1/2 lbs. sugar in 1 pt. of water; cool and add to liquor. Add 1 oz. yeast and the juice of 2 lemons; cover and ferment 7 days. Pour into gal. jar leaving sediment off. Boil 1-1/2 lbs. sugar in 1 pt. of water, cool and add to liquid. Cover and let it set until all fermenting has ceased. Bottle immediately.

Red Beet Wine

Grind 5 lbs. of beets with skins on. Boil with 1 gal. of water until tender; strain through cloth. Add 2-1/2 lbs. of sugar and 1/2 t. of pepper to beet water; boil 15 min. and cool. Spread 1 oz. yeast on toasted wheat bread. Put liquid into crock. Place toast on top of liquid, yeast side up. Let stand 12 days at room temperature. Strain and bottle.

Fruit jars can be used with lids in place of bottles. This is a crystal clear garnet color wine everyone was proud to serve guests.

Rhubarb Wine

Clean, cut and weigh 4 lbs. of rhubarb. Place in crock, add the juice of 1 lemon. Add 2 t. of almond extract. Pour 4 qts. boiling water over ingredients. Stir and cover. After three days, strain into clean container, add 3-1/2 lbs. sugar to liquid; dissolve completely. Add 1/2 cake yeast, stir, and cover and skim skum off every day. After one week bottle tightly.

A. Anderson
Dresser, WI

Home Brew

Prohibition didn't stop many from making their own beer. This recipe is quite potent but it still was bottles in picnic bottles, the large brown half gallon size.

Dissolve:
1 can   malt
11 lg.c. sugar — in hot water rinsing out the malt can.

Add enough cold water to make 10 gals. total. Dissolve yeast in warm water and add to the rest when bubbly. Let stand 3 days or until bubbles are gone. Bottle immediately.

Old Time Home Brew

Recipe from the old country and still in use during the depression.

1 can	malt	3 sm.	potatoes, diced
4 gal.	water	1-1/2	cakes yeast
5 lbs.	sugar	1 lb.	raisins

Put malt in a large kettle and heat with sugar until dissolved. Add some water if necessary to keep from burning it. Add rest of water, stir well. When mixture is luke warm add yeast, potatoes and raisins. Set in a warm place to work. Ready to bottle in seven or eight days or when bubbles are gone.

Home Rendered Lard

"We put a large roaster of fat pork in the oven for all afternoon because if you did it slowly or baked it all day at low temperature it stayed nice and white.

It is also dangerous because as the lard melted it had to be poured into jars and sealed immediately.

Preserved Pork

My husband said his Mom fried down all of their pork piece by piece and put it in crocks and poured hot lard over it. And it kept that way. Therefore, most of it was sliced up because it had to be cooked entirely. The hams and bacon were hung in the salt sacks in the summer kitchen or smoke house.

They also kept eggs in crocks of salt in the basement. They kept a long time that way".

Audry Samplaruski
Chetek, WI

Making Your Own Laundry Soap

6 lbs.   clean grease, strained
1 can   lye
5 c.   soft water
2 T.   borax
2 T.   sugar
1/2 c.   ammonia

Melt fat in a large iron or enamel pan. (Not aluminum) Should be 6 pt. Cool to 80F and combine 13 oz. can of lye with 5 c. of water in enamel pan, stirring slowly with long wooden paddle. Long paddle is necessary to keep from splashing hands. Cool to 70F. Add lye water gradually to fat, stirring slowly for 10 min. Stir until mixture is creamy, then add borax, sugar and ammonia. Mix well and pour into shallow pans or cardboard box. Cool slowly for 24 hrs. Remove from mold and cut with string into bars. Stack and let dry for two weeks. If properly dried, soap should be white and will float.

Mrs. R.H. Brunzlick
Augusta WI

When the going got tough, it was obvious that the tough got going. The women of the Great Depression proved it as the following recipes will show.

When absolutely nothing could be found in the pantry to even begin to make an evening meal for the family, the following was put together, and because they were hungry, it was considered good. At any rate, there was nothing left over.

Pan dripping were put into the cast iron pan. Flour was added and stirred until it was a dark golden brown. Salt and pepper and a clove and bay leaf were added. Cold water was poured in to make a creamy consistency. Any leftovers in the pantry were added. If the soup still was too lean, because there were never may leftovers, old dried crusty bread from the crock was gathered and crumbled into the soup. This gave it a thicker consistency and made an evening meal.

Another recipe when nothing was available and it was mealtime was begun with a pan of boiling water. Seasonings and dry bread was added. Then beaten eggs were poured in while stirring vigorously. At least no one in this house went to bed hungry.

It wasn't often we had cake flour in the house, so we made our own. To each cup of flour we removed one tablespoon and added 2 tablespoons of cornstarch.

Menomonie WI

Sliced bread made its appearance in the early thirties. I recall mother exclaiming, "What will they think of next!" Also, about that time chocolate flavored oleo made a brief visit, only good on graham crackers. It didn't make the best-seller list.

Iris Martin
Sheboygan WI

My Favorite Recipe _____

Miscellaneous Foods

Lefsa

Making lefsa is no less than a fine art. Not everyone can produce a perfect product without first learning it from the professional, the Scandinavians.

Working as a team is easiest, but not necessary, one rolling to the precision thin quality it needs and the other baking to exact doneness.

Overbaking will result in a dry lefsa and is not acceptable to a good lefsa baker.

Lorraine's Lefsa

Day 1: Boil enough peeled baking potatoes to make 16 c. of hot riced potatoes.

Add: 1 c.   butter, melted
        1 can   evaporated milk
        3-1/2 t. salt

Mix well and let cool in a cool room overnight. Do not cool in refrigerator.

Day 2: Mix 4 c. potato mixture with 2 c. flour at a time.

Roll very thin using pastry cloth and sock on rolling pin. Use just enough flour to prevent sticking. Bake on hot lefsa griddle. Put on towels and cover with towels.

Lorraine Peterson
Menomonie, WI

Easy-To-Make Lefsa

This recipe has been handed down through the years and is used by young homemakers today.

Measure 8 c. mashed potaotes which have been salted while cooking.
Add: 1 c. whipping cream
          1/2 c. softened butter
Mix well, cover with waxed paper pressed down on potato mixture. Cover with towel and refrigerate overnight.
(Continued next page)

(Continued from last page)

Mix 2 c. potatoes with almost 1 c. flour. Knead well. Form into 8 egg shapes. Put on plate in refrigerator. Roll out on floured board. Bake on lefsa griddle. Yields 32 delicious moist lefsa. (Submitted by Laurel Madsen, Menomonie WI)

Red Beet Eggs

These attractive naturally colored eggs often graced an Easter breakfast or lunch. Boil eggs gently for 20 min. Peel under cold water immediately. Add to juice of canned pickled beets. Let stand overnight or several days.

Another recipe calls for cooking beets until tender. Remove skins.

Dissolve:

1/2 c.	brown sugar	1 c.	vinegar
1 c.	water	1 stick	cinnamon
3 or 4	cloves	1 t.	salt

Bring to a boil and pour over beets. Next day remove beets and add the hard boiled eggs.

Pickled Gizzards or Eggs

These made excellent lunches and provided a change from the unusual.

Bring to a boil:

1/2 c.	sugar	4 c. white vinegar
2 T.	pickling spices	1/2 t. salt
		some onion rings

Let cool. Pour cold brine over cooked and cooled gizzards or eggs. Brine may be saved and eggs added after gizzards are used.

Lorraine Peterson
Menomonie, WI

The water in Dead Lake, Arkansaw, Wisconsin, was clean and pure and it held an abundance of nice, large freshwater carp. Prepared with expertise, they made excellent food. They were skinned, a line of dark meat was removed from each side, and then were stuffed before baking. An absolute sumptuous meal remembered by George LaPean, of Menomonie, Wisconsin.

Super Duper Ice Cream

Mix 1/4 c. cornstarch in 1 qt. of hot milk. Stir constantly and let come to a boil Chill.

Beat: 2   eggs, well

Add: some   vanilla
           1/4 t.   salt
           3/4 c.   sugar

Add to a pt. of cream; add all to milk mixture. Freeze in freezer.

This ice cream is absolutely excellent and does not need a topping.

Toppings for commercial ice cream, easy to prepare and delicious.

Caramel Ice Cream Topping

Mix: 1 c.   brown sugar
           4 T.   flour
           1/4 t.   salt

Add: 3/4 c.   water

Cook and stir until thick and smooth. Pour hot over ice cream and sprinkle with crushed salted peanuts.

Fudge Sauce

Mix together: 1-1/2 c. sugar
                1 c.   cocoa
                1 c.   water
                1 t.   vanilla
                some   salt

Boil 15 min. Serve hot or cold.

Myrtle's Fatiman

This delicious ethnic delicacy dates back many years and is still finding it's way into the holiday preparations of Scandinavian heritage homes.

Beat very thoroughly: 8 egg yolks
1 egg white

Add: 4 T. sugar — Beat again very well.

Add: 4 T. cream
1 t. ground cardamom

Mix in: 2 c. cake flour (Or 1-1/2c. flour and scant 1/2c. cornstarch)
pinch salt

Mix and roll out very thin. Cut into diamond shapes and fry in hot fat until very light brown. Drain on paper towels. Dust with powdered sugar.

Myrtle Collins
Moorhead, MN

Listy

A Sczeck name for a similar confection calls for eggs, cream, sugar, and flour mixed well. Dough should be stiff. Knead for 7 to 10 min. on floured board. Proceed with instructions like Fatiman.

Marie Larson
Rice Lake, WI

Proportions and method of assembling are like Fatiman.

171

Mushrooms

Another one of the items the good earth provided which the women took full advantage of was mushrooms. They provided variety to meal planners in the country. Sorels were gathered in Wisconsin in the fields and on the banks under trees by the dish pan full.

They were canned and processed for winter use and were fried in butter or lard for summer noon meals.

Puffballs were common in Minnesota where they were gathered in the morning by the pails full, sliced and fried in butter and served on large platters. Bread, butter and coffee accompanied this delicacy.

Mushrooms were also dried in some areas and used to thicken potato soups, and probably other soups as well.

Taffy

The entire family enjoyed taffy making and it was popular when there was a good supply of syrup on hand and an extra cup of sugar.

Boil: 2 c.   light syrup
          1 c.   sugar
          1 t.   vinegar — until hard ball stage.

Remove from heat and add soda and vanilla. Pour on buttered platter to cool. When cool pull until white and ropy. Cut into bite size pieces with a scissors. Butter hands generously before pulling taffy.

Betty Eaver
Holcombe, WI

* * *

<u>Delicious Molasses Taffy</u> is made with the same method using:-

2 c.	sugar	1/2 c.	water
3 T.	butter	2 t.	cider vinegar
1/4 t.	salt	1/2 c.	molasses

Butter hands generously before pulling.

The Earl Hammonds of Menomonie, Wisconsin, remember that their two brood sows had a very special duty on the farm. They had to produce enough little piglets to pay the taxes on the land.

And because of their considerable station in the animal hierarchy on the farm, they were treated as such. Their rations included skim milk daily.

But Verna Hammond remembers well that there were also pigs to be butchered and meat to be cured and smoked.

To avoid shrinkage, the smoking was done very slowly using hardwood maple. It took about two weeks to complete the smoking process because it was not finished until no redness was left in the center of the meat. The Hammonds purchased their 80 acres in 1933 for $5,250, and it has been a very good, productive farm, they recall.

I bleached mash and feed bags with lye water, making sheets, pillow cases, children's pajamas and underclothes for the family. I even made my husband work pants and shirts for awhile using heavier type cement bags, and dyed them gray.

N. Kellnhofer
Medford WI

MY FAMILY TREASURY OF HEIRLOOM RECIPES

Date Recorded_____

Part II

More From Your Kitchen Today

Introduction

This collection of easy, everyday recipes is dedicated to Micki Paske and all the other young brides who need nutritious, economical meals in a hurry. The philosophy behind these recipes is one of basic, down-to-earth good eating, using a minimum of preparation time, and maximum nutrition and economy. Most of the economy (and nutrition) comes from buying foods in their most natural state. You pay highly for processing (which strips vitamins) and packaging of foods and in the long run don't really save time. Studies show that the time you save in the kitchen with convenience foods is spent in extra minutes or hours of shopping. If you stock your shelves with basic staples you can prepare a great variety of recipes at a minimum cost.

Consider this cookbook a creative "guide" to cooking. Some recipes do not give exact amounts because they come from creative cooks who use a dab of this and a dribble of that. You also will become creative as you use them, and will delight in the joy of not measuring. In these cases, tasting as you go is a requirement.

Jan Van Amber Paske
Home Economist

Shopping Hints

Following are some shopping hints that help make the entire business of feeding your family easier, cheaper, and less time-consuming:

Planning your menus a week at a time around weekly supermarket specials saves time and money. A local newspaper pays for itself when you utilize the ads. Shop several stores that are within reasonable distance, picking up specials at each one. Staples vary a great deal in price from one store to the next, and you'll soon learn what to buy where. Shop during least busy hours - morning or early afternoon are best.

Food coops or certain health food stores are an economical source of many staples that become expensive in the supermarket simply due to packaging. Wheat germ, bran, oatmeal, whole grain flours, and baking yeast are good examples of this. I even get fresh and Parmesan cheeses through a food coop at a terrific savings. The larger your family the more worth your while this becomes. (Cheeses can also be purchased more reasonably at cheese factories.)

Another reasonable source of some foods are the day-old baskets at some supermarkets. Fruits and vegetables which you plan to use within a few days are good buys, especially items such as bananas or avocados which need to be very ripe for use in some recipes anyway. Day-old French bread is an excellent buy as it's heated before serving anyway, and bread stuffing is best day old when it's begun to dry out. Toast, French toast, grilled sandwiches, and bread pudding are other uses of day old bread. Some stores also mark down meats from the day before, and they are very wholesome and can be used right away or frozen. You usually have to shop early in the morning to find these bargains as they are limited and disappear quickly.

Many generic products are fine, especially gelatins, onion soup mix, or anything you're combining with other ingredients. They are sometimes half the price of the brand name product, and may even be made by that same company! Do compare ingredients, however, as some use low quality cholestorol causing fats, such as coconut, palm and cottonseed oils. Avoid products with a list of fats saying "one or more of the following:". Nutrition is more important than savings.

Don't waste money on high calorie, low nutrition foods. These are usually the most expensive anyway. The money you save can be spent at the fruit and vegetable counter to put life and variety into your meals. Try a bunch of grapes for snacks instead of a box of potato chips. Remember that the more variety you can get into your diet, whether it's grains, fruits, or vegetables, the healthier you will be.

Stock up at farm markets in the fall - 50 lbs. of onions keep all winter in the garage; a bushel of squash keeps 'til temperatures drop below freezing. (The remaining squash can then be baked, scooped out, and frozen.)

NOTES:

Baking Hints and Substitutions

Use wire whisk for blending dry ingredients.

Oil is healthier and quicker to measure and blend than shortening.

Always make double or triple batches to be frozen and used later. (A big time-saver with casseroles as well - often the leftovers are even better.)

To clean counter from bread dough or other messy tasks: scrape clean with spatula; squeeze water over remaining stuck on dough and allow to stand to soften; wipe clean.

A spatula is also handy to lift dough from counter while working with bread dough.

Don't be afraid to substitute healthier or less expensive ingredients, particularly for family use only - milk for cream, yogurt or cottage cheese for sour cream, Monterey Jack cheese for Mozzarella (we like its flavor even better), sour milk for buttermilk.

Mock Sour Cream

Process in blender 'til smooth:
1/2 c.	cottage cheese
1/4 c.	buttermilk
1 T.	oil
1 t.	lemon juice
1/8 t.	salt

Evaporated Milk

Process in blender:
1 c.   nonfat dry milk] Makes 1-1/3 c. or the
1-1/4 c.water   ] equivalent of an 11 oz.
                          can.

Sweetened Condensed Milk

Bring to a boil very high heat:
1 c.	sugar
1/2 c.	water
1/3 c.	butter

Whirl in a blender with: 1-1/3 c. nonfat dry milk. Cool and refrigerate overnight before using. Makes 1-1/3 c. or the equivalent of an 11 oz. can. (Microwave: heat sugar, water and butter 1 min. on high. Stir to dissolve sugar.) This may also be made without the butter, and with half the sugar if you're counting calories.

Buttermilk

Measure 1 T. vinegar or lemon juice into 1 c. measure; add reconstituted nonfat dry milk to make 1 c. Allow to sit at room temperature to clabber.

178

Low-Calorie Whipped Topping

Soften 1 t. Knox gelatin in 2 t. water for 5 min. Stir 1/4 c. nonfat dry milk into 1/2 c. skim milk in saucepan. Heat to simmering; add softened gelatin and stir to dissolve. Add 1/2 t. vanilla and 1 T. sugar. Chill until it begins to thicken. Beat until very thick and light. Store in refrigerator for use within several days or freeze for longer storage.

Homemade Yogurt

Combine 2 c. whole milk, 2 c. reconstituted nonfat dry milk, and 1/4 c. dry milk powder in saucepan and heat 'til bubbles appear around edge (scalding); do not let mixture boil. Remove from heat; pour into bowl; cool to lukewarm (110F-115F). Stir in 2 T. plain yogurt; cover and let stand in warm place about 10 hrs. (May put in oven which has been preheated to warm and turned off.) Options: May use all skim milk if desired; may add 1/2 T. dissolved Knox gelatin for firmer texture.

Use yogurt to replace half the mayonnaise in salad dressings for fewer calories and more calcium.

Yogurt Fruit Whip: Process 1 c. yogurt, 1/2 c. cut-up fresh fruit, and 1 t. honey in blender.

Low-Cal Marmalades or Yogurt Toppings

Apricot-Apple Spread: Combine 1 can (6 oz.) frozen apple juice concentrate, 1-1/2 c. apple juice (or water), and 8 oz. dried apricots, finely snipped, in saucepan and simmer 25 min. or 'til apricots are very tender and most of liquid is absorbed. Remove from heat. Stir in 1/2 t. almond extract and 1/4 t. cinnamon. Cool and store in refrigerator. Delicious on homemade bread or toast.

Pineapple-Orange Marmalade: Combine 1 can (20 oz.) crushed pineapple, 1 c. orange juice, 1-1/2 T. cornstarch, 1 t. vanilla, and a dash of cardamom in saucepan and bring to a boil, stirring 'til thickened. Cool and store in refrigerator.

Cooking and Health Hints

Canned chicken or beef broth thickened with cornstarch adds more flavor than creamed soups to casseroles. It is also usually free from additives.

Use your pressure cooker for speedy meals, especially homemade soups. Gives them that cooked all day flavor.

No need to peel tomatoes for canning – clean, remove stem end, quarter, and process in food processor 'til desired size. Skins are not noticable after canning, and little bits of tomato are more palatable to most children than larger pieces.

Add parsley to chili, soups, BBQ's, and stews for extra vitamins for picky eaters. Finely grated carrot can also be added to BBQ's, chili, and spaghetti. Grated zucchini is a meat extender.

No need to eliminate meat altogether for health purposes – just serve one portion per person and have plenty of salad, vegetables, potatoes, whole wheat rolls, and a nutritious dessert.

Buy hamburger on special; brown 5 lbs. at a time with onion, celery, green pepper, and parsley; freeze in 1 lb. packages to use for quick spaghetti, BBQ's, goulash, etc.

Ground turkey is almost fat-free and healthier than ground beef. It can be substituted for ground beef in most recipes. No need to drain fat off!

Boil potatoes in jackets, covered with water. Store in refrigerator for quick fried potatoes on busy nights. Can be a great emergency meal with eggs, toast, and fruit. (Don't peel before frying.)

To eliminate salt on garlic bread, make seasoned butter with garlic powder and Parmesan cheese or thyme.

APPETIZERS AND BEVERAGES

My Favorite Recipe _____

Cheese Fondue

Heat together: 1   recipe thick white sauce
                     1/2-1 c. cheddar cheese, cubed

Toast in oven: 1   loaf French bread, cubed
                     some   garlic salt or powder
                     some   butter, melted

Broccoli Dip

1 can   mushroom soup
1 jar   garlic cheese spread (or log)
1 pkg.   frozen broccoli, cooked and chopped

Combine and heat. Serve in chafing dish with Fritos to dip.

Crab Cream Cheese Spread

Place 2 (8 oz.) pkgs. of cream cheese side by side on a fancy plate. Cover with flaked crab or mock crab sticks (from deli). Drizzle Hoffman House Shrimp Sauce over all. Serve with assorted crackers.

Guacomoli Dip

1   avocado   3/4 c.   sour cream
8 oz.   cream cheese   1 T.   lemon juice
some   garlic salt to taste

Blend. Spread on dinner plate and chill. Just before serving layer on top any combination of: shredded lettuce, green onions, sliced green olives, chopped tomatoes, shredded cheddar cheese, green pepper, mushrooms. Serve with tostada chips.

Sue's Taco Dip

8 oz.   cream cheese
8 oz.   sour cream
2 T.   Worcestershire sauce
1/2 pkg.   taco seasoning

Combine and spread on large platter. Serve with toppings
as (Guacamoli Dip) above.

Joyce's Cheese Squares

Combine: 1/2 lb.   cheddar cheese, shredded
         1 can   onion rings
         some   salad dressing to hold together

Spread on cocktail rye bread. Bake at 350F for about 15
min. or 'til cheese melts. Serve hot.

Curry Dip for Raw Veggies

1/2 c.   mayonnaise   ]
1/2 c.   sour cream or yogurt]
1 t.   curry   ] Mix
1/2 t.   tumeric   ] and
1/4 t.   chili powder   ] refrigerate.
1/4 t.   ginger   ]
1/4 t.   paprika   ]
some   salt and pepper   ]

Dottie's Vegetable Dip

1/4 c.   onion, chopped   ]
1/2 t.   salt   ]
1/2 t.   celery salt   ] Process
1/2 t.   pepper   ] in
1/4 t.   tabasco   ] blender
1 t.   caraway seed   ] 'til
1 t.   dry mustard   ] smooth.
1 t.   Worcestershire   ]
1 pt.   cottage cheese   ]
1 pt.   Hellmans mayonnaise   ]

Curried Popcorn

Heat 1/4 c. butter, 2 t. curry, and 1 t. salt 'til bubbly. Drizzle over 1 c. popcorn popped. Add peanuts if desired.

Parmesan Popcorn: Substitute 2-4 T. Parmesan for curry.

* * *

For a quick, delicious Mid-Eastern snack, stuff prunes with cream cheese.

Thelma's Orange Julius

6 oz.	frozen orange juice concentrate
1 c.	milk
1 c.	water
1/4 to	
1/2 c.	sugar
1 t.	vanilla
10	ice cubes

Process in blender 30 seconds. Serve immediately.

For breakfast on the run, use milk in place of water and add 4 eggs. Garnish with orange slices.

Sparkling Punch

1 qt.	orange juice
1 qt.	unsweetened pineapple juice
1 qt.	white soda
1 qt.	ginger ale

Serve in chilled punch bowl with ice ring made with juice, if desired.

Bertie's Hot Cider

1 qt.	apple cider	] Put spices in
2 t.	whole allspice	] bag or tea ball.
2 t.	whole cloves	] Simmer 20 min.
4 sticks	cinnamon	]

Russian Tea

Simmer 10 min:

1 stick	cinnamon	]	Let stand
1-1/2 t.	whole cloves	]	1 hr.
1/4 c.	honey	]	Strain.
1 c.	water	]	

Steep 1 min: 6 c.   boiling water
              2 T.   black tea

Strain tea and add with spiced honey water:

2/3 c.   orange juice
1/4 c.   lemon juice

Reheat and serve hot. Garnish with thin orange slices.

My Favorite Recipe _____

BREADS

My Favorite Recipe _____

BREADS

Easiest Ever Caramel Rolls

Dissolve in large bowl:
1-1/4 c.	warm water	1 T.	dry yeast (1 pkg.)

Add:
1/3 c.	dry milk	2 T.	sugar
1/4 c.	oil	1 t.	salt
2	eggs	2 c.	flour

Stir well with wire whisk. Add 2 c. more flour and stir well with wooden spoon. Cover, rise 'til double, 1 hr. (Or microwave on lowest power 10 min., turning bowl after 5 min.) Stir down, knead a few strokes with a little flour, and turn out onto floured surface. Roll into 12x8" rectangle. Melt 1/2 stick butter in 9x13" pan. Spoon some of butter onto dough and spread to cover surface. Sprinkle dough and pan with brown sugar. Sprinkle dough generously with cinnamon, and raisins, if desired. Roll up, jelly roll fashion, and cut into 12 slices. Place in pan, rise 1/2 hr. (or 10 min. in microwave) and bake 20 to 30 min. at 350F. Invert on platter and serve immediately.

Rolls or Buns: Form into balls 1/2 the size of desired end product, rise and bake as above.

Pizza Crust: Make roll recipe, eliminating sugar and eggs, and 1 to 2 c. less flour. After rising spread out on cooky sheet, bake at 400F on lower oven rack 'til slightly browned; spread with sauce (below); top with Monterey Jack cheese, mushrooms, green pepper, onion, and Parmesan Cheese; bake 'til cheese melts and browns slightly.

Pizza Sauce: Mix 1 sm. can each tomato sauce and tomato paste and stir in oregano, basil, thyme, fennel seed, and garlic powder to taste.

189

Overnight Crescent Rolls

Combine: 1 c.   hot water
1/2 c.   sugar
1/2 c.   shortening, butter, or oil
1/3 c.   dry milk powder
1 t.   salt

Sprinkle on to dissolve: 1 pkg.   yeast

Beat in: 3   eggs
4 c.   flour (may use all or part
              whole wheat)

Cover; let stand all night. Divide into 2 parts; roll each part into a circle and cut each circle in 8 pie-shaped pcs. with pizza cutter. Roll up beginning with wide end. Bake in 350° oven 10 min. 'til golden. Great for breakfast or brunch as they can be ready so quickly.

Milwaukee Biscuits

Mix: 1 pkg.   yeast — in 1/2 c. water.
4 c.   warm water
1-1/3 c. dry milk
1 c.   mashed potato
3/4 c.   sugar (or 1/2 c.)
1 c.   oil
2 t.   baking powder
2 t.   salt (optional)
1 t.   soda

Add flour (6 c.) to make soft batter. Let rise 'til covered with bubbles. Add flour to make stiff dough. Knead in bowl 'til smooth and elastic. Refrigerate. As needed pinch off for biscuits. Rise 1 hr. Bake at 425F for 15 min. Makes 6 doz. Dough keeps up to a week in refrigerator.

These taste more like dinner rolls than biscuits, and besides being conveniently available in the refrigerator, they are healthy, containing no eggs and less fat and sugar than most rolls. Can also be used for cloverleaf rolls, pecans rolls, Swedish tea rings, etc.

No-Knead Oat Raisin Loaves

Combine: 1-1/2 c. boiling water
   1 c. oats, uncooked
   1/2 c. molasses
   1/3 c. oil
   1 T. salt

Dissolve:
1/2 c. water
2 pkg. dry yeast

When oats are lukewarm, add: the yeast above
            2   eggs
            1 c. raisins

Stir in gradually: 5-1/2 c. flour, about
          (may use part whole wheat)

Cover and refrigerate at least 2 hrs. When dough has chilled, shape into 2 loaves; place in greased loaf pans; cover and rise in warm place 'til double, about 2 hrs. Bake at 350F for 1 hr. Makes terrific toast.

Brown Nut Bread

Stir together: 2-1/4 c. whole wheat flour
      1-3/4 c. unbleached flour
      2 t. baking soda
      1 t. salt

Combine: 2   eggs
   2 c. sour milk (1 T. vinegar/c. sweet milk)
   1/2 c. molasses
   1/3 c. honey
   2 t. orange or lemon peel, shredded

Combine all with: 1 c. nuts, chopped
        3/4 c. raisins

Bake in 2 loaf pans at 350F for 55 min. Remove from pans and cool on wire rack.

Zucchini or Pear Bread

3	eggs
1 to 2 c.	sugar
1 c.	oil
1 T.	vanilla
2 c.	zucchini, grated or unpeeled pear, chopped
3 c.	flour (may use 1/2 whole wheat)
1 t.	salt
1 t.	soda
1/2 t.	baking powder
1 T.	cinnamon
1 c.	raisins or nuts

Combine as for quick bread and bake in 3 med. loaf pans for 1 hr. at 325F.

Use less sugar for pear bread and if you're adding raisins.

This goes quickly in a food processor. Chop pear; add liquids and spices; process; add dry ingredients and process only 'til moistened.

Banana Nut Bread

Beat with wire whisk: 4 eggs

Add and beat: 1/2 to 1 c. sugar and 1 c. oil

Stir in:
1 t.	cinnamon
1-1/2 t.	cloves
2 t.	soda
1/2 t.	salt
2 c.	flour (may use 1/2 whole wheat)
1-1/2 c.	nuts, chopped
1-1/2 c.	raisins

Fold in: 6 ripe bananas, mashed. Bake in 2 loaf pans for 1 hr. at 325F.

Food processor: Insert metal blade. Mash bananas; add eggs, oil, sugar, and spices; process. Add flour, nuts and raisins, and process only 'til moistened.

This is an old Southern recipe and the best banana bread I've ever tasted.

Whole Wheat Baking Mix

6 c.	whole wheat flour
3 c.	unbleached flour
1-1/2 c.	dry milk
1 T.	salt
1 c.	sugar
1/2 c.	wheat germ
1/4 c.	baking powder

Mix with wire whisk in lg. bowl. Store in covered glass jar. Use in recipes below.

Breakfast Cake From Mix

Beat together:	2	eggs
	1/3 c.	oil
	1/3 c.	honey, if desired
	1-1/2 c.	water

Stir in:	4 c.	wheat mix
	1 c.	raisins

Spread in 9x13" pan. Sprinkle with brown sugar, cinnamon, and nuts. Bake at 350F for 25 min.

May use part orange juice for water and add grated orange peel.

Wheat Nut Bread from Mix

Combine:	1	egg
	1-1/4 c.	water

Stir in 'til moistened:	4 c.	mix
	1/2-1 c.	nuts, chopped

Bake in loaf pan for 50 min. at 350F.

Whole Wheat Corn Bread

Combine:
1 c.	cornmeal
1/2 c.	whole wheat flour
2 T.	dry milk
2 T.	wheat germ
2 t.	baking powder

Combine:
1	egg
1 c.	buttermilk or sour milk
1/4 c.	oil

Stir dry ingredients a third at a time into liquid ingredients. Bake in well-greased 8" pan or corn muffin tins 20 to 30 min. at 375F.

Bake double batch in well-greased preheated cast-iron skillet and cut in wedges to serve.

Serve with maple syrup and fruit and cottage cheese salad for a low sodium, low cholesterol lunch.

Mixed-Grain Corn Bread

Combine:
1-1/3 c.	cornmeal
2/3 c.	whole wheat flour
1/4 c.	wheat germ
2 T.	sesame seed
2 T.	soy grits (optional)
2-1/2 t.	baking powder
1/2 t.	soda
1/2 t.	salt

Beat together:
1	egg
1/4 c.	oil

Add:
2 c.	buttermilk

Stir liquids into dry ingredients, blending 'til moistened. Bake in well-greased 10" preheated cast iron skillet at 400F for 25 min.

194

Blueberry Corn Muffins

Mix:
1/4 c.	butter, soft
1/4 c.	white sugar
1/4 c.	brown sugar
1	egg
1/2 c.	milk
1/4 t.	salt
1/4 t.	nutmeg

Stir in lightly:
1 c.	flour
1/2 c.	cornmeal
2 t.	baking powder

Toss together:
1/2 c.	blueberries
1-1/2 t.	flour

Add blueberries to barely moistened batter (do not overmix). Fill 12 muffin cups and bake for 20 to 25 min. at 400F. May use fresh, frozen or canned blueberries.

Banana Bran Muffins

Combine:
3/4 c.	buttermilk
1/2 c.	ripe banana, mashed
1	egg, beaten
2 T.	oil
4 T.	molasses

Stir together:
1 c.	whole wheat flour
3/4 c.	miller's bran
1 t.	soda
1/4 t.	salt

Combine all and add: 3/4 c. raisins

Spoon into 12 greased muffin pans. (Do not use paper baking cups.) Bake at 375F for 25 to 30 min.

Miller's bran is unprocessed wheat bran and is available at supermarkets or health food stores. Refrigerator bran muffins are better with miller's bran than ready-made bran cereal as there is no processing or additives. Cheaper, too, because you use less.

Fat-Free Banana Bran Muffins

Combine: 2 c.   bran
1 c.   whole wheat flour
1-1/2 t. baking powder
1/2 t.   soda
1 c.   sunflower seeds
1 c.   raisins
1/4 c.   sesame seeds

Combine: 1   egg, beaten
1 c.   buttermilk
1/4 c.   molasses
2   ripe bananas, mashed

Add liquid to dry ingredients and stir only until moistened. Bake in greased muffin cups 25 to 35 min. at 350F.

These muffins are great for breakfast on the run because they are so substantial. They are quite heavy, but can be made lighter by using 1 c. bran instead of 2.

Quick Oil Biscuits

Stir together: 2 c.   flour
1 t.   salt
3 t.   baking powder

Combine in measuring cup. Don't stir:
1/3 c.   oil
2/3 c.   milk

Add liquids to dry ingredients; stir with fork 'til mixture rounds up. Knead a few strokes. Pat out to 1/2" thick on ungreased cooky sheet; cut in diamonds (crosswise one way and diagonally the other), and bake at 450F for 10 to 12 min.

Drop biscuits: Increase milk to 3/4 c. or so. Drop tablespoonfuls onto cooky sheet and bake as above. Serve hot with Honey Butter.

Honey Butter

1 c.   butter, soft
1-1/4 c. honey
1   egg yolk

Combine in deep bowl. Beat 10 min. Store in refrigerator.

Instant Biscuits

Bring to room temperature 2 c. of self-rising flour and 1 c. fresh cream or sour cream. Blend to form a soft dough; if it becomes too stiff, add 1 t. water. Pat out to 1/2 " thick on cooky sheet. Cut into diamonds and bake at 450F for 10 to 15 min. Serve hot with butter and Apricot or Pineapple Marmalade.

To use regular flour in place of self-rising, add 1-1/2 t. baking powder and 1/2 t. salt to each cup of flour.

Wheat Muffins or Biscuits

Combine with wire whisk:

1 c.	whole wheat flour
3/4 c.	unbleached flour
1/4 c.	unprocessed bran
4 t.	baking powder
1/2 t.	salt (optional)

Beat together:

1 lg.	egg
1 c.	milk
1/3 c.	butter, melted or oil

Stir liquid ingredients into dry just until moistened. Bake in muffin cups or preheated cast iron skillet (well greased) at 400F for 20 min. or so. Like a biscuit in flavor - good with soup.

NOTES:

Sam's Whole Wheat Pancakes or Waffles

Mix:
- 3 c.   whole wheat flour
- 1-1/2 t.   salt
- 3 t.   baking powder
- 1/2 c.   dry milk

Beat: 3   egg yolks

Add and stir into dry ingredients:
- 3 T.   oil
- 3 c.   water

Beat to soft peaks and fold in: 3   egg whites

Bake on greased griddle and serve hot with Wisconsin maple syrup!

These pancakes are the lightest I've ever tasted and the secret is in beating the egg whites separately, so don't skip that step.

Finnish Pancake

Blend in blender:
- 3   eggs
- 2 c.   milk
- 1 t.   salt

Add and blend:
- 2-3 t.   sugar
- 1 c.   flour

Melt 1/3 c. butter in 9x13" pan at 350F. When it sizzles add batter and bake for 45 min. Serve with strawberries and cream.

NOTES:

Orange Pancake Puff

Boil in lg. saucepan: 1 c.   water
                                    1/2 c.   butter
                                    1/2 t.   orange peel, grated

Add and stir into ball: 1 c.   pancake mix
(or 1 scant c. flour, 1-1/2 t. baking powder, 1/2 t. salt)

Add, one at a time, and beat: 4 eggs

Spread batter on bottom and sides of 2 generously greased 9" pie plates. Bake at 400F for 15 min., then at 300F for 10 min. or 'til golden. Cut into wedges and serve with choice of toppings. Serves 8.

Creamy Fruit Topping

Combine: 1 c.   sour cream
         1 T.   honey
         1 t.   orange peel, grated
         1/4 t.   cinnamon

Fold in: 1 can   fruit cocktail, drained

Buttery Peach Topping

1 can   peaches (16 oz.)
2 T.   butter
1 T.   orange juice
1 t.   orange peel, grated
2 t.   cornstarch
1/8 t.   nutmeg

Combine in saucepan. Boil 2 min. Serve warm over Pancake Puff.

NOTES:

Chippewa Fry Bread

Mix:
    2-1/2 c. flour
    1-1/2 T. baking powder
    1 t.   salt

Mix:
    3/4 c.   warm water
    1 T.   dry milk
    1 T.   oil

Combine liquid and dry ingredients, stirring 'til smooth.
Knead 4 to 5 times. Let rest 10 min. Form into 8 balls;
flatten to 8 to 10". Make hole in center of each round,
lightly flour, stack and cover. Heat 1" oil in skillet.
Cook one at a time for 1 to 2 min. on each side. Drain
and sprinkle with cinnamon and sugar.

This is an Indian recipe that is fun for kids to help
with. The legend is that the hole is put in the center of
the bread to let the evil spirits out.

Faith's Individual Coffee Cakes

Mix like pie crust:
    3 c.   flour
    5 t.   baking powder
    1/4-3/4 c.   sugar
    1 stick   butter

Mix in only to moisten:
    2   eggs
    3/4 c.   milk
    1 t.   almond flavoring
                  (or vanilla or lemon)

Drop by large spoonfuls onto cooky sheet. Bake at 375F
for 15 to 20 min. Frost with butter icing.

NOTES:

Delores' Danish Coffee Cake

First layer:
1 c.	flour
1 T.	sugar (optional)
1/2 c.	butter
2 T.	water

Mix as for pie crust. Roll in ball and divide in half. Pat into 2 long strips 12x3", side by side on baking sheet.

Second layer:
1/2 c.	butter
1 c.	water
1 t.	almond (or vanilla extract)
1 c.	flour
3	eggs

Bring butter and water to boil in saucepan. Remove from heat; add flavoring. Add flour and beat fast. When smooth add 1 egg at a time, beating after each 'til smooth. Spread 1/2 evenly on each strip. Bake 1 hr. at 325F 'til top is crisp and brown. Frost with butter frosting. (optional - top with chopped nuts.)

This has become a family favorite of ours and is so good that I have never served it without someone asking for the recipe.

Coffee Cake Loaf

Cream: 1 c. shortening   2 c. sugar

Add 1 at a time, beating well: 4 eggs

Combine: 3 c. flour   1/2 t. salt
         1 t. baking powder

Add alternately with flour: 1 c. milk

Put 1/2 of batter in bottoms of 2 greased bread pans. Sprinkle with 2/3 of cinnamon mixture. Top with remaining batter and remaining cinnamon. Bake at 350F for about 1 hr. Keep in refrigerator 2 to 3 weeks. Slice thin and spread with butter (optional) to serve.

Cinnamon mixture: 2 T.   cinnamon
                      7 T.   sugar

201

Lemon Bread

```
6 T.        butter, melted
1 c.        sugar
2           eggs
1/2 c.      milk
1 rind      lemon, grated (or 1 T. lemon juice)
1 t.        baking powder (heaping)
1-1/2 c.    flour
1/2 c.      nuts or slivered almonds
```

Mix in order given. Bake in 2 loaf pans for 1 hr. at 350F. Let stand 15 min. Turn out and while still warm spoon over juice from 1 lemon combined with 1/2 c. sugar.

Microwave Boston Brown Bread

```
1/2 c.      unbleached flour
1/2 c.      whole wheat flour
1/2 c.      cornmeal
1 t.        soda
1/2 t.      salt
1/2 c.      raisins
1 c.        buttermilk or sour milk
1/3 c.      dark molasses
1/4 c.      oil
```

Blend ingredients together well. Line bottom of 2-cup measure with circle of wax paper. Pour in half the batter. Cover with vented plastic wrap.

Microwave at 50% powder 6 to 8 min., rotating cup 1/2 turn after 3 min. Bread is done when center springs back when touched lightly and no unbaked batter appears on sides of cup.

Cool 5 to 10 min. Remove from cup; microwave second loaf with remaining batter. Serve warm. To reheat, place slices on plate, cover lightly with plastic wrap, and microwave on high 30 t 60 seconds.

Pita Bread

1 pkg.   yeast
1-1/4 c. water
3 c.   flour (part whole wheat)
2 t.   salt

Mix as bread dough. Divide into 6 balls. Knead each 'til smooth and round; flatten with rolling pin to 1/4" thick and 5" diameter. Cover with towel; rise 45 min. Arrange rounds upside down on baking sheet. Bake at 500F for 10 to 15 min.

This is an especially good diet recipe as there is no fat or sugar included. To serve, cut in half and fill with your favorite chopped vegetables and cheese, and top with sour cream or yogurt.

The pita dough balls are perfect for small children to knead and roll out, and when baked they can choose their own chopped vegetables to fill them. A rainy-day activity!

Breadsticks or Pretzels

Dissolve: 1-1/3 c. warm water
       1 pkg.   yeast

Beat in: 3 T.   oil
       1 T.   honey
       1 t.   salt
       1 c.   whole wheat flour

Stir in about 2 c. white or whole wheat flour, to make soft dough. Rise 'til double, 45 min. Stir down by beating 25 strokes. Turn out on floured board. For breadsticks, divide into 24 pieces. Roll each into 9" rope and place on greased cooky sheet. Brush with beaten egg and sprinkle with coarse salt or sesame seeds. Bake at 400F 'til golden brown and crisp, about 15 min.

Pretzels: Divide dough into 12 equal parts. Roll each into 18" rope and twist into pretzel shape. Continue as for breadsticks.

Cheese Pretzels

Dissolve: 3/4 c.   warm water
          2 t.   sugar
          1 t.   yeast

Blend in 'til smooth: 2 c.   flour
                         1/2 c.   cheese, grated

Knead. Form into pretzels. Brush with beaten egg, sprinkle with coarse salt. Bake at 425F for 15 min. Serve warm with mustard.

This recipe is also fun for children and makes a terrific snack.

Oven French Toast

4 slices white bread, 1" thick
3   eggs
3/4 c.   milk
1 T.   sugar
1/4 t.   salt

Arrange bread in ungreased 9x13" pan. Mix remaining ingredients and pour over bread. Refrigerate overnite. (Or, dip and bake immediately.) Bake on greased baking sheet 8 min. on each side at 500F.

Evelyn's Breakfast Cornmeal Pudding

Combine, heat to scalding: 1/4-1/2 c. sugar or honey
                              1 t.   salt
                              3 T.   butter
                              3 c.   milk

Combine, stir into above: 1 c.   cornmeal
Cook 'til thickened, stirring.   1 c.   milk
Cover, cook 5 min., stirring.

Beat: 3 eggs

Stir a small amount of hot cornmeal into eggs, then back into cornmeal, stirring constantly. Cook covered over low heat 5 min. Spoon into serving bowls, sprinkle with nutmeg. Serve warm with milk or cream.

Oatmeal with Stewed Apples

Bring to boiling: 2 c.   water

Stir in: 2 c.   old-fashioned oats

Add: 1   apple, chopped or thinly sliced
          1/4 t.   cinnamon
          1/4 t.   salt

Cook covered 10 min. Serve up hot with honey and milk.

Swiss Oatmeal

2 c.   uncooked oats
1-1/4 c.   milk
3/4 c.   raisins
1/2 c.   orange juice
1/3 c.   wheat germ
1/4 c.   honey
1/4 t.   salt

Combine all ingredients in covered refrigerator bowl.
Refrigerate overnite or up to 4 days. Serve as is with
milk. Great alternate for hot oatmeal in summer.

Homemade Hot Rice Cereal

Blend brown rice in blender a few spoonfuls at a time to
make 1/2 c. rice powder. Bring 2 c. water and dash of
salt to a boil. Stir in with wire whisk 2/3 c. powdered
milk and 1/2 c. rice powder. Lower heat, cover, and
simmer 8 to 10 min.

Microwave: Bring water to a boil, stir in dry milk and
rice. Cook 1 min. at 50% power, stir; then 9 min. at 30%
or 'til thickened, stirring once or twice.

NOTES:

Quick and Easy Granola

Heat: 1/2 c.   oil
           1/2 c.   honey

Add: 1 T.   vanilla
          1/2 t.   salt

Pour over: 10 c.   old-fashioned oats

Toss until well coated. Toast in large shallow pan 15 min. at 350F. Stir and bake 5 min.; stir and bake 5 min. more if needed. When cool add your family's choice of trail mix, raisins, currants, nuts, sunflower seeds, sesame seeds, wheat germ, dates, coconut, etc. Store in an airtight container. Serve with milk, or plain as a snack.

Hint: Measure oil first and then the honey; the oil coating the cup will allow the honey to slip out easily.

My Favorite Recipe _____

COOKIES

My Favorite Recipe _____

COOKIES

Peanut Raisin Balls

3/4 c.   peanut butter, plain or crunchy
3 T.   honey
1/2 c.   dry milk powder
1/2 c.   raisins

Put peanut butter and honey in food processor with metal blade. Process about 3-5 seconds. Add dry milk and process 'til mixture forms a ball on blades. May add raisins before ball forms and finish processing with raisins, or transfer to bowl and knead raisins in. Roll into balls and refrigerate 1/2 hr. before serving.

Variations: Carob powder or chips may be added in place of or in addition to raisins. May also be rolled in coconut or crushed cereal before refrigerating.

If you don't have a food processor or you do have children who want to do something in the kitchen, all the ingredients can be worked together with hands in a bowl.

Choco-Date Balls

Blend: 1/2 c.   chunky peanut butter
         1/4 c.   carob powder
         2 t.   vanilla

Mix in: 2 c.   oatmeal

Cook 1 min: 1/4 c.   butter
                  2/3 c.   honey

Add: 1 c.   dates, snipped
         the   oatmeal mixture

Shape into balls and chill.

Molasses Butterball Cookies

Beat: 1 c.   butter

Beat in: 1/4 c.   molasses

Add: 2 c.   flour
           2 c.   walnuts, chopped

Shape into 1" balls. Bake at 325F for 20 min. Cool and roll in powdered sugar.

Basic Oatmeal Cookies

Beat with wire whisk: 2   eggs

Beat in: 1 c.   oil

Beat in: 1 c.   sugar
         1 t.   soda
         1 t.   salt
         1 t.   almond (or vanilla)

Stir in with wooden spoon: 1-1/2 c. flour
                            3 c.   oats

Drop onto ungreased sheets. Bake for 10 min. at 350F.

Variations: Use almond flavoring and add coconut. Use vanilla flavoring and add chocolate or carob chips, raisins, carob powder, or nuts, whatever your family prefers.

NOTES:

Pepparkakor (Swedish Ginger Cooky)

Cream:
- 1 c. butter
- 1-1/2 c. sugar

Add:
- 1 egg
- 2 T. molasses
- 2 t. soda in a bit of hot water
- 1 t. cinnamon
- 1 t. ginger
- 1 t. salt
- 1/2 t. cloves

Add: 3-1/4 c. flour

Roll thin and cut out with cooky cutters. Bake for 10-15 min. at 300F.

This is our traditional Christmas cooky, as is, with no frosting. It is a crisp cooky as opposed to the more familiar holiday gingerbread cookies. If you wish to adorn it, sprinkle with colored sugar before baking.

Other times of year the dough can be rolled in balls and pressed with a glass dipped in sugar before baking. They disappear fast, so plan to make a double batch!

For an even quicker cookie, spread dough in 2 3" strips crosswise on cooky sheet. Bake for 8-10 min. at 325F, or 'til desired doneness; longer for crisp cooky, shorter for soft cooky. Cut each strip crosswise into 1" slices before removing from cooky sheet (a pizza cutter works well for this). This strip cooky method can be used with any cooky dough; for peanut butter flatten with fork dipped in sugar, for chocolate chip sprinkle chips on flattened dough and press in lightly.

NOTES:

211

Amish Cookies

Combine: 1/2-1 c. white sugar
1 c.   powdered sugar
1/2-1 c. butter
1 c.   corn oil

Add; beat well: 2 eggs

Add: 4-1/2 c. flour
1 t.   almond (or vanilla)
1 t.   cream of tartar
1 t.   soda
1 t.   salt

Chill overnite. Roll into balls; press with glass dipped in sugar. Bake at 350F for 12 min. or 'til slightly browned.

May substitute 1 c. wheat germ for 1 c. of the flour.

Coconut Drops

Mix: 1 c.   unsweetened coconut
1 T.   creme de cocoa

Beat 'til stiff: 3   egg whites, room temp.
1 T.   brown sugar

Fold coconut into egg whites. Drop onto greased cooky sheet. Bake for 7-10 min. at 400F. Refrigerate to store.

Sesame Crisp Cookies

Blend: 1/2 c.   oil   1/2 c.   honey
1   egg

Stir in: 1/4 c.   milk   1/2 c.   dry milk
1-1/4 c. oatmeal   1 c.   whole wheat flour
1 t.   cinnamon   1/4 t. salt
3/4 c.   sesame seeds
1/4 c.   raisins or chocolate chips

Drop onto cooky sheet. Bake 10 min. at 350F-375F.

Peanut Butter Treats

Combine: 1   egg   1/2-1 c.   honey
          1 c.   oil   1/4 c.   water
          1 t.   salt   1 t.   vanilla

Combine: 3 c.   oats
          1 c.   whole wheat flour
          3/4 c. wheat germ

Stir together; add: 1 c.   peanut butter pieces
                     1/2 c.   sunflower nuts

Drop onto greased cooky sheets; flatten. Bake for 15-20 min. at 350F.

Variation: Substitute carob chips for peanut butter pieces.

Chocolate Peanut Butter Bars

Heat to boiling: 1/2 c.   corn syrup or honey
                  1/4 c.   brown sugar (optional)
                  1/8 t.   salt

Stir in: 1 c.   peanut butter

Stir in: 3 c.   Cheerios
         6 oz.   chocolate or carob chips
         1 t.   vanilla

Pat into buttered 9" pan. Refrigerate 1 hr. or 'til firm. Cut into bars. May use corn flakes in place of Cheerios, in 9x13" pan.

NOTES:

Date Oatmeal Bars

Combine: 2 c.   dates, chopped
         1 T.   flour

Add; simmer 10 min: 1 c.   hot water

Add: 1 t.   vanilla

Combine: 1 c.   brown sugar
         1 c.   flour
         1 t.   soda
         2 c.   oats

Add gradually: 1/2 c.   butter, melted

Spread half of oatmeal mixture in 8x12" pan. Cover with
dates, then sprinkle with remaining oatmeal. Pat with
spoon. Bake at about 350F for 20 min. or so.

Oatmeal Fruit Bars

Combine: 2 c.   flour
         2 c.   oats
         1/2 c.   honey
         3/4 c.   butter, melted

Press half in greased 9x13" pan.

Cook 10 min: 1/2 c.   honey
         2 T.   lemon juice
         1 c.   applesauce
         1 c.   dates
         1 c.   raisins

Spread over crust. Top with other crumbs. Bake for 20-25
min. at 400F.

NOTES:

Banana Whole-Wheat Walnut Bars

Beat together:
1/2 c.	oil
1/2 c.	honey
1/4 c.	brown sugar (optional)
2	eggs
1 t.	vanilla
3 med.	bananas, mashed

Stir in:
1-2/3 c.	whole wheat flour
1 t.	baking powder
1/2 t.	soda
1/2 t.	salt
1/4 c.	milk
1 c.	nuts, chopped

Bake in 9x13" pan for 30 min. or 'til toothpick comes out clean.

Pumpkin Nut Bars

1/2 c.	shortening		1 c.	brown sugar
1 c.	flour		1/2 t.	soda
1/2 t.	baking powder		1 t.	cinnamon
1/4 t.	ginger		1/4 t.	nutmeg
2/3 c.	pumpkin		2	eggs
1 t.	vanilla			

Combine all ingredients and beat for 2 min. Fold in 1/2 c. chopped nuts. Bake in 9x13" pan for 20 to 25 min. at 350F. When cool spread with Orange Frosting.

Orange Frosting: Blend 'til smooth: 2 T. butter, 1-1/4 c. powdered sugar, 1 T. grated orange peel, and 2 T. orange juice.

NOTES:

Sue's Rhubarb Bars

Mix as pie crust: 1 c.   flour
                          5 T.   powdered sugar
                          1/2 c.   margarine

Pat in 9x13" pan. Bake for 12-15 min. at 350F.

Combine: 2   eggs, beaten
          1-1/2 c. sugar
          1/4 c.   flour
          3/4 t.   salt
          2 c.   rhubarb

Spread on crust. Bake another 35 min. at 350F.

Dream Bars

Cream: 1/2 c.   brown sugar
          1/2 c.   butter

Blend in:1 c.   flour

Press into ungreased 9" pan. Bake for 10-15 min. at 375F.

Beat: 2   eggs

Beat in: 3/4 c.   brown sugar
          1 t.   vanilla

Mix in: 2 T.   flour
          1/2 t.   baking powder
          1/2 t.   salt

Spread over crust. Add: 1 c.   walnuts
                        1-1/2 c. coconut

Bake for 15-20 min. longer.

Carrot Brownies

Melt: 1/2 c.   butter

Stir in well: 1-1/2 c. brown sugar

Beat in: 2   eggs

Beat in: 2 c.   flour
        2 t.   baking powder
        1/2 t.   salt
        2 c.   carrots, grated

Pour into 2 8" greased pans. Sprinkle with 1/2 c. chopped nuts. Bake for 30 min. at 350F. (May process in blender as with Carrot Cake.)

Lucy's Lemon Squares

Blend: 1 c.   flour
        1/2 c.   butter
        1/4 c.   powdered sugar

Pat into 8" pan. Bake for 20 min. at 350F.

Beat: 2   eggs
        1 c.   sugar
        1/2 t.   baking powder
        2-1/2 T.   lemon juice
        1/4 t.   salt

Pour over crust and bake another 20-25 min.

NOTES:

Apple Oatmeal Bars

Mix as pie crust: 1 c.   oatmeal   1 c.   flour
                    1/2 t.   salt   1/2 t.   cinnamon
                    1/2 c.   butter

Pat 1/2 in 8x10" pan.

Spread on: 2-1/2 c. apples, chopped
           1/2 c. sugar

Top with remaining oatmeal. Dot with butter. Bake for 35 min. at 350F.

Peanut Butter Secrets

Melt: 1 c.   butter

Mix in: 2/3 c.   wheat germ
        1-1/4 c. dry milk

Blend in with spoon: 1 c.   peanut butter
                   1-1/2 c. powdered sugar
                   1 c.   graham cracker crumbs

Spread in 9x13" pan and press down firmly to form smooth surface. Melt 1-1/2 c. carob chips and spread evenly over peanut butter mixture. Refrigerate to harden carob.

Bonnie's Praline Strips

Layer on greased, sided cooky sheet: 24 whole graham crackers.

Boil 1 min: 1 c.   brown sugar
           1 c.   butter
           1 c.   nuts

Pour over crackers. Bake 10 min. at 350F. (Watch so they don't burn.) Cut or break in pieces.

This is a wonderfully easy Christmas candy-type bar, perhaps not nutritious, but absolutely delicious. I've made it with soda crackers in an emergency, and it is equally good, but becomes soggy after some storage.

DESSERTS

My Favorite Recipe _____

DESSERTS

In recipes where a range of sugar amounts is given (such as 1-2 cups) use whatever your family's taste prefers. If you've been cutting back on super-sweet desserts and snacks, the lesser amount will taste sweet enough. If you want to start cutting back, just decrease the amount of sugar in baked goods over a period of time, and taste buds will adjust to a more natural level of sweetness. Most recipes will tolerate cutting the sugar in half, especially if there are fruits added which provide natural sweetness (such as bananas, apples, raisins, etc.) You can also substitute concentrated apple juice for liquids to eliminate even more sugar if desired.

In most of the baked goods recipes cooking oil has been substituted for the shortening, for health reasons (less saturated fat), and for speedier measuring and mixing. Most recipes will tolerate substituting oil, in fact, the result is often a moister product. Try it with your own recipes, starting with replacing half the shortening with oil. You can measure slightly less oil than you would shortening.

No-Roll Pie Crust

Combine in 9" pie pan:

1-1/2 c.	flour
1-1/2 t.	sugar
1 t.	salt

Whip with fork:

| 1/2 c. | oil |
| 2-3 T. | milk |

Pour oil into flour; mix; pat evenly in pan. Use as any other pie crust.

Rolled Oil Pie Crust

| 1 c. | flour (minus 1 T.) | 1/4 c. | oil |
| 2 T. | milk | pinch | salt |

Combine all ingredients in bowl and blend lightly. Form gently into ball. Roll out between sheets of waxed paper into a 10" circle. Remove waxed paper, fold dough in half and then in half again. Transfer to 9" pie plate. Unfold dough and fit into plate, tucking and fluting edge. Double recipe if top crust is also desired.

Mom Paske's Rhubarb Pie

Combine: 2   eggs, beaten
        1 c.   sugar
        1 T.   flour (heaping)
        1 T.   butter

Mix in: 2 c. strawberry rhubarb, diced(the red thin kind)

Put in crust. Add lattice-work top crust. Bake at 375F for 10 min., then at 350F for 45 min. Delicious!

Pumpkin Pie

1-3/4 c. cooked pumpkin or squash
1-3/4 c. milk

3	eggs	2/3 c.	brown sugar
2 T.	white sugar	1-1/4 t.	cinnamon
1/2 t.	salt	1/2 t.	ginger
1/2 t.	nutmeg	1/4 t.	cloves

Combine all ingredients in blender. Process 'til well mixed. Pour into No-Roll Pie Crust in 9" pan. Bake at 400F-425F for 45 to 55 min., or until knife comes out clean. Serve slightly warm with whipped cream.

Also good baked in custard cups with no crust. Top with a mixture of butter, brown sugar, and nuts, if desired.

Apple Betty Pie

In 9" pan: 5 c. apples, sliced

Sprinkle on: 1/4 c. orange juice

Combine: 1/ c.   brown sugar
        1/2 c.   flour
        1/2 t.   cinnamon
        1/2 t.   nutmeg
        1/4 t.   salt

Cut in: 1/4 c.   butter

Sprinkle topping over apples. Bake at 350F for 40-45 min. Serve warm with ice cream or whipping cream.

Cranberry Surprise Pie

In 10" pie pan: 2 c.   raw cranberries
                   1/3 c. sugar
                   1/2 c. nuts, chopped

Melt and cool: 1/2 c. butter
                 1/4 c. Crisco

Beat: 2 eggs

Add bit by bit: 1 scant c. sugar while heating

Mix in: the   butter, melted
         1 c.   flour
         1/8 t.   salt

Pour batter over cranberries. Bake at 325F for 50-60 min. Serve with ice cream.

Judy's Low-Cal Pineapple Pie

2 env.   unflavored gelatin
2 c.   crushed pineapple, drained
1-1/3 c. cottage cheese
1 t.   vanilla
1 t.   any other extract
4 t.   sugar

Soften gelatin in pineapple juice; heat. Place all ingredients in blender and process thoroughly. Pour into 8" pie pan and refrigerate until firm. Serve with whipped topping if desired.

Donna's Impossible Coconut Pie

4   eggs
1/2-1 c. sugar
1 c.   coconut
2 t.   vanilla

1 stick butter
1/2 c. flour
2 c.   milk
1/2 t. salt

Place all ingredients in blender. Process 1-2 min. until mixed. Pour into well-buttered 10" pie plate. Bake at 350F for 30-35 min. You will have a crust, a custard-type filling, and a browned coconut topping.

Crazy Cake

1/3 c.	cocoa
3 c.	flour
2 c.	sugar
2 t.	soda
1 t.	salt
2 T.	vinegar
2 t.	vanilla
3/4 c.	salad oil (scant)
2 c.	cold water

Combine dry ingredients. Make 3 wells; into one pour vinegar, another vanilla, the third the oil. Pour water over all. Mix well with wire whisk. Bake 30 min. at 350F in 9"x13" pan. Very delicious.

Children love to make this cake. May also be mixed right in baking pan to eliminate bowl.

Broiled Topping: Combine 1/2 c. soft butter, 1 c. brown sugar, 1/2 c. nuts, 1 c. coconut, 1/3 c. light cream or evaporated milk. Spread on warm cake. Broil 3 min. or 'til bubbly.

Microwaves well. Use bundt pan and follow directions for cakes in microwave cookbook.

Karen's Apple Cake

2	eggs
1/2 c.	oil
1-2 c.	sugar (or 1/2 c. honey)
dash	salt
2 t.	cinnamon
2 t.	soda
2 t.	vanilla
4 c.	apples, chopped
2 c.	flour
1 c.	nuts, chopped (or raisins)

Mix all ingredients together and bake in 8x16" pan for 45 min. at 350F. Serve warm with or without glaze on top. (Mix powdered sugar and a bit of hot water.)

(Continued on next page)

Food Processor: Chop apples in work bowl with blade. Add eggs and process. Add oil, sugar seasonings, and vanilla; process. Add remining ingredients and process 'til just mixed.

May use 1 c. oat flour in place of 1 c. white. (Process 1-1/2 c. oatmeal in blender.) May also replace 1/2 the flour with whole wheat.

For fancy cake, increase recipe by 1/2 (3 eggs, 3/4 c. oil, etc.) and bake in well-greased Angelfood cake pan. Sprinkle top with 1 t. cinnamon, 1/3 c. sugar, and 1/2 c. nuts combined before baking. Cool, invert, and cut in wedges to serve. One of my children chooses this easy cake for his birthday every year!

Carrot Cake

Process in blender:
4		eggs
1 c.		oil
2-3 lg.		carrots, in chunks

Blend in:
1-2 c.	sugar
2 t.	cinnamon
2 t.	soda
1 t.	salt
1 t.	vanilla

Stir into 2 c. flour in bowl or pan and bake in 9x12" pan at 325F for 45 min. to 1 hr.

Cream Cheese Frosting: Beat well: 1 8 oz. pkg. cream cheese, 1/2 stick butter, 1 t. vanilla, powdered sugar to stiffen.

Lemon Glaze Frosting: Beat together in bowl with wire whisk: 2 T. melted butter, 2 T. lemon juice, 1 c. powdered sugar. Delicious, and fewer calories than cream cheese frosting!

Cream Cheese Honey Frosting: Whip 8 oz. cream cheese and add honey to taste.

Whole Wheat Carrot Cupcakes

Blend: 1 c.   white sugar
            1 c.   brown sugar
            1 c.   oil

Add: 1 t.   vanilla

Beat in 1 at a time: 4 eggs

Beat in: 2 c.   whole wheat flour
        1/3 c.   dry milk powder
        1 t.   soda
        1 t.   baking powder
        3 t.   cinnamon

Stir in: 3 c.   carrots, finely shredded

Bake in muffin tins at 350F for 40 min. Makes 12 plump muffins.

Blender directions: Process oil and 3 cubed carrots; add eggs and vanilla, and process the remaining ingredients.

Pumpkin Bars or Cake

1 c.   pumpkin (or leftover squash)
1-2 c.   sugar
4   eggs
1 c.   oil
2 c.   flour
1 t.   soda
1 t.   baking powder
1/2 t.   salt
2 t.   cinnamon
1 c.   nuts, chopped

Combine all ingredients, stirring in nuts last. Bake in 10x15" cooky sheet for bars, or 13x9" pan for cake, for 25 min. at 325F. Top with Lemon Glaze (see Carrot Cake recipe) or Cream Cheese Frosting: 3 oz. cream cheese, 6 T. butter, 1 t. vanilla and 3 c. powdered sugar.

Delores' Oatmeal Cake

Set 20 min: 1 c.   oatmeal
1-1/2 c. boiling water

Cream: 1/2 c.   shortening
          1 c.   brown sugar
          1 c.   white sugar
          2   eggs

Add: the   soaked oatmeal
          1-1/3 c. flour
          1 t.   soda
          1 t.   cinnamon
          1/2 t.   salt

Bake in 9x12" pan for 30 min. at 350F.

Frosting: Combine: 6 T.   butter, melted
                  1/4 c.   milk
                  1/2 c.   brown sugar
                  1 c.   coconut
                  1/2 c.   nuts

Spread over baked cake and broil 'til bubbly.

Margaret's Rhubarb Cake

Cream: 1/2 c.   shortening
          1 to 1-1/2 c. brown sugar

Add: 1   egg

Combine: 2 c.   flour
         1 t.   soda
         1 t.   salt

Add alternately with flour: 1 c. sour milk (or buttermilk)

Fold in: 1-1/3 c. rhubarb, in small pieces

Sprinkle with: 1/4 c.   sugar
              1 t.   cinnamon

Bake at 350F for 35-40 min. Serve warm with whipped cream.

Hurry-Up Frosting

1 c.	sugar	2 T.	cocoa
1/4 c.	butter	1/4 c.	milk

Bring to rolling boil in saucepan; cook 2 min. Remove from heat. When lukewarm, beat until thick enough to spread.

Blueberry Cobbler

Mix:
- 1-1/2 c. sugar
- 1/2 c. flour
- 1 t. salt

Add:
- 2 qts. blueberries
- 3 T. lemon juice

Pour into greased 9x13" pan. Dot with 3 T. butter. Bake at 400F for 15 min. or 'til hot and bubbly.

Combine:
- 2 c. flour
- 4 t. baking powder
- 2 T. sugar
- 1 t. salt
- 1/4 c. dry milk powder

Cut in: 1/2 c. shortening

Stir in with fork: 2/3 c. water
1 egg, slightly beaten

Drop into hot berries making 12 biscuits. Bake 20 min. 'til browned. Serve warm with cream or ice cream.

To substitute cooking oil for shortening, just stir it into water and egg, then add all together to dry ingredients.

Strawberry Shortcake

Prepare biscuit topping from Blueberry Cobbler. Bake in 9" pan for 20 min. at 400F or 'til golden brown. While still slightly warm, cut in squares, split, fill with fresh sliced sweetened strawberries, add top, more strawberries, and finish off with mounds of freshly whipped cream. Almost a meal!

Peach Pandowdy

In 8" dish:	6 c.	fresh peaches, sliced
	3/4 c.	sugar
	2 T.	tapioca
	1/4 t.	salt
Dot with:	2 T.	butter
Combine:	1 c.	flour
	3 T.	sugar
	2 t.	baking powder
	1/2 t.	salt
Cut in:	3 T.	butter
Stir in:	1/2 c.	milk

Drop in 6 mounds on peaches. Bake at 375F for 50 min. or 'til browned. Serve warm with cream or ice cream.

Pineapple Custard

1 c.	unsweetened pineapple juice
1/4-1/2 c.	sugar
6	eggs
dash	salt
1/2 t.	vanilla

Simmer pineapple juice with sugar for 15 min. Refrigerate. Beat eggs and salt at high speed for 5 min. or 'til light and fluffy. At med. speed, slowly beat in cold pineapple mixture, then vanilla. Bake for 45 min. in 2 qt. casserole placed in shallow pan of hot water (or 'til set). Serve warm. Serves 6.

Dodie's Baked Pineapple

Mix: 1/2 c.   sugar
              2 T.   flour

Beat and add: 3   eggs

Add: 1 can   crushed pineapple

Put in greased baking dish.

Top with: 4 slices bread, in pieces
           1 stick butter, in pieces

Bake at 350F for 1 hr.

Rice Pudding

Cook 7 min: 1 c.   water
           1/2 c.   rice
           1/4 t.   salt

Add, cook 1-1/2 hrs. on low heat:
           1 qt.   milk
           1/4 c.   butter
           some   lemon or orange peel (optional)
           1 stick cinnamon (optional)

Add: 2   eggs, beaten
          1/2 c.   sugar
          1/2 c.   raisins
          1/2 t.   vanilla

Serve warm or chilled, sprinkled with cinnamon or nutmeg.
(Leave citrus peel and stick cinnamon in and remove just
before serving.)

Apricot Whip

1 c.   cottage cheese
2/3 c.   milk
1/4 c.   dried apricots
2 T.   sugar
1/2 t.   almond extract

Process in blender until smooth. Serves 3-4.

EGGS, FISH AND CHEESE

My Favorite Recipe _____

EGGS, FISH AND CHEESE

Meatless meals are inexpensive and healthy, but usually take more time to prepare. Here are some quick ones.

Skillet Zucchini Parmigiana

Sauté on both sides:
4 med.	zucchini, sliced lengthwise 1/4" thick
1 clove	garlic
some	cooking oil

Layer with zucchini in skillet, making several layers:
some	garlic salt
some	pepper
some	oregano
1-1/2 c.	spaghetti sauce (I use tomato sauce and add oregano, basil, thyme and fennel)
1/3 c.	Parmesan
1/2 lb.	Mozzarella, sliced thin or grated

Cover and heat on low 'til cheese is melted and mixture is heated through. Serves 4. Great with garlic bread and a tossed salad.

* * *

The following lasagna recipe is fantastic because you don't cook or brown anything before you put it together. With all the cheese in lasagna you don't really need the meat. Whole wheat lasagna noodles makes it even better.

NOTES:

Spinach Lasagna

Combine in bowl:

1 lb.	cottage cheese
1 c.	Mozzarella, shredded
1	egg
1 pkg.	spinach (10 oz.)
3/4 t.	oregano
1/8 t.	pepper

Layer 3 times in 9x13" pan:

32 oz.	spaghetti sauce (I use tomato sauce with oregano, basil, thyme & fennel seed added.)
9	uncooked lasagna noodles
and	cheese mixture (above)

Pour 1 c. water around edges. Cover with foil. Bake at 350F for 1 hr. and 15 min. Remove foil. Top with 1/2 c. shredded Mozzarella and bake 'til cheese is melted.

Three Cheese Strata

Sauté:

4 oz.	mushrooms
1/2 c.	onion, chopped
1/2 t.	marjoram
1 T.	butter

Butter and cube: 6-12 slices day old bread (I use 12 for family, fewer for a ladies luncheon.) Spread 1/2 in bottom of lg. baking pan or individual ramekins. Top with mushrooms.

Combine & spread over mushrooms:

1/2 c.	cheddar cheese, shredded
1/2 c.	Swiss or Monterey Jack, shredded
1/4 c.	Parmesan
1 t.	dry mustard — Top with remaining crumbs.

Beat together and pour over cubes:

6	eggs
1-1/2 c.	milk
1/2 t.	salt

Refrigerate several hrs. or overnite. Bake at 350F for 20 min.

234

Broccoli Cheese Pie

Cook together 5 min., drain:
1-1/2 lb.broccoli, peeled and sliced thin
2/3 c. onion, minced

Combine:
4   eggs, slightly beaten
1-1/4 c. milk
1 t.   salt
dash   pepper
few-drop hot pepper sauce (optional)
1 T.   parsley, minced
1/8 t.   nutmeg
2/3 c.   Swiss cheese, shredded (Monterey Jack is good)

Stir in vegetables and turn into well-buttered 10" pie plate. Sprinkle with 1/4 c. Parmesan cheese. Bake at 350F for 30-35 min. Cool 10 min. before cutting. Good with sliced tomatoes sprinkled with Italian dressing and hot rolls or biscuits.

Quick Garden Quiche

Combine in 10" pie plate:
2 c.   broccoli or cauliflower, cooked and chopped
1/2 c.   onion, chopped
1/2 c.   green pepper, chopped
1 c.   cheddar cheese, shredded

Beat until smooth:
3   eggs   1-1/2 c. milk
3/4 c.   Bisquick   1 t.   salt
1/4 t.   pepper

Pour over vegetables. Bake until golden brown, 35 to 40 min. Let stand 5 min. before cutting.

NOTES:

235

Quiche Lorraine (Modified)

Combine: 1/4 c.   dry onion soup mix
        3   eggs, slightly beaten
       1-1/4 c. milk
       2 T.   parsley
       1 T.   pimento (optional)

Pour in greased pie plate. Bake at 350F for 40 min. Ten min. before done, top with slices of Mozzarella, Swiss, or Monterey Jack cheese. (I double everything but the soup mix for a lower salt content.)

Spinach Ricotta Tart

Prepare and bake 10 min: 1 pie shell

Sauté: 1 sm. onion, minced

Cook, drain, and squeeze out moisture: 2 pkg.   spinach
                                   (10 oz. each)

Combine in lg. bowl:
3   eggs, slightly beaten
1 ctn.   ricotta (or cottage) cheese (15 oz.)
1 c.   light cream or milk
1/2 c.   Parmesan cheese
1/2 t.   salt
1/4 t.   nutmeg
dash   pepper

Add spinach and onion. Pour into baked pastry shell. Bake at 350F for 50 min. or 'til browned and set. Serve with tossed salad and cornbread.

NOTES:

Onion Pie

Sauté until transparent: 1 lg.   sweet onion
                          2 T.   butter

Combine and press into 9" pan:
6 T.   butter, melted
1-1/2 c. Saltine cracker crumbs

Beat together: 3   egg   1-1/4 c. milk
               1/2 t. salt   dash   pepper

Spoon onions over crust. Pour eggs over all. Sprinkle
with 1/2 c. grated cheddar cheese and paprika. Bake at
350F 'til firm.

Sicilian Frittata

Sauté until tender: 2 T.   oil
                      2   potatoes, sliced
                      1/2 c.   onion, chopped
                      1/4 c.   green pepper, chopped
                      2 cloves garlic, minced

Add and cook 5 min. covered: 2 c. broccoli, chopped

Beat together: 6   eggs
                      1/4 c.   Parmesan cheese
                      1/4 c.   water
                      1/2 t.   basil
                      1/4 t.   salt

Pour over vegetables in pan. Cook on low 10-15 min. 'til
set. Grate 1/2 c. any kind of cheese over top before
serving.

Potatoes are more interesting and nutritious when fried
with skins left on.

Pasta Primavera Salad

Mix in lg. bowl:
- 1/2 c. oil
- 1/3 c. lemon juice
- 2 cloves garlic, halved
- 1 t. salt
- 1 t. mustard
- 1/2 t. sugar

Add and refrigerate: 8 oz. cooked spaghetti, warm (whole wheat is best)

Remove garlic and toss in before serving:
- 3 stalks broccoli, cut up (sm.)
- 5 oz. Mozzarella (or other) cheese, in strips
- 1/4 c. Parmesan
- 7 oz. tuna (canned)

Great summer supper with bread sticks and sliced tomatoes.

Mushroom Omelet

Saute fresh sliced mushrooms and chopped onion in butter. Beat 2 eggs per person with 1 T. water per egg and add to mushrooms in pan. As omelet cooks on underside, lift with spatula to allow uncooked egg to run under. When almost cooked throughout turn off heat, halve or quarter, and turn. Grate Monterey Jack cheese on top and serve when cheese is melted.

Alfalfa Sprout Omelet

Melt butter in frypan. Beat 2 eggs per person with 1 T. water per egg and pour in pan. Spread sprouts loosely over eggs. Continue cooking omelet as in mushroom omelet, above, and adding grated cheese before serving.

Tuna Eggplant Skillet

Sauté: 1 lg.   eggplant, peeled and cubed
       1   onion, chopped
       1/2   green pepper, chopped
       3 T.   butter

Add: 1 can   mushroom soup
       1 can   tuna, drained
       1 c.   cheese, grated
       1 t.   garlic salt
       1/4 t.   pepper
       4-5 drops Tabasco sauce (optional)
       2 t.   Worcestershire sauce
       3 c.   brown rice, cooked (1 c. uncooked)

Stir together and heat thoroughly. Top with 1 c. more
cheese. Sprinkle with paprika, if desired. Cover and
heat 'til cheese melts. Serves 6 generously.

Tuna Tomato Salad

Combine and chill: 2 cans   tuna
                   1 c.   celery, chopped
                   1/2 c.   walnuts, chopped
                   1/4 c.   sliced stuffed olives
                   1 T.   lemon juice
                   1/2 c.   sour cream
                   1/4 t.   seasoned salt (optional)

Cut in thirds and spread open: 1 tomato per serving.
Place portion of tuna mixture on each tomato. Over top,
pour mixture of lemon juice and parsley.

NOTES:

239

Joyce's Crunchy Tuna Salad

Combine. Chill 1 hr:

1 c.	salad dressing
1 T.	lemon juice
1 t.	soy sauce
some	garlic salt - to taste
1 c.	celery, sliced
2 T.	onion, chopped
2 cans	tuna, drained (sm.)

Fold in just before serving:

1 pkg.	frozen peas
1 c.	chow mein noodles

Serve on lettuce leaf, sprinkled with 1/4 c. toasted slivered almonds, if desired.

Tomato Tuna Cups

Toss together:

1 can	tuna, drained (7 oz.)
1/2 c.	celery, chopped
1/3 c.	green pepper, chopped
2 T.	onion, chopped
1/2-1 t.	curry
1/4 t.	salt
dash	pepper
1/2 c.	mayonnaise

Cut 6 tomatoes into 6 wedges each, almost to base. Place on lettuce cup and fill with tuna. Serves 6.

Tuna Vitamin Sandwich Spread

1 can	tuna (13 oz.)	Combine all
3 lg.	carrots, finely grated	ingredients,
1 med.	apple, unpeeled and finely chopped	mixing well.
1 sm.	green pepper, minced	
1 c.	celery, minced	Great for
1/2 c.	mayonnaise	sandwiches
1/2 c.	nuts, chopped	or to stuff
1/4 c.	wheat germ	tomatoes.
1 T.	Worcestershire sauce	
1 T.	lemon juice	

Food processor: Process vegetables in work bowl with blade; add remaining ingredients and process 'til just mixed.

HOTDISHES

My Favorite Recipe _____

Skillet Beef and Noodles

Brown: 1 lb.   ground beef or turkey

Add: 1 T.   mustard
      1/4 t.   oregano, basil, thyme
      1 pkg.   onion soup mix
      4 oz.   dry uncooked noodles or broken spaghetti
                (whole wheat is good)
      1 can   tomatoes
      3/4 c.   water

Cover, simmer 20 min. Garnish with grated cheese or Parmesan cheese if desired.

Tagliarini

Brown: 1 lb.   ground beef

Add: 1-1/2 t. salt
      1/8 t.   green pepper
      1 t.   oregano
      1 med.   onion, chopped
      1 clove   garlic, chopped
      2 cans   tomatoes (1 lb. each)
      1 can   corn with juice
      1 can   ripe olives, drained (optional)
      1-1/2 c. noodles, uncooked

Cook 25 min., stirring occasionally. Remove lid. Cook 10 to 15 min. more. Sprinkle with 1/4 c. Parmesan cheese before serving, if desired.

Super Duper

8 oz.	noodles	1 lb.	hamburger
1 c.	onion, chopped	1 c.	celery, chopped
1 can	mushroom soup	1 can	water

Combine in 8x12" baking dish. Bake at 350F for 1-1/2 hrs.

Easy Lasagna

Brown:	1 lb.	hamburger
	2 T.	onion, chopped
	1/2 c.	celery, diced

Add and simmer:	1 t.	oregano
	1/2 t.	salt
	dash	pepper
	2 cans	tomato sauce (15 oz. each)
	1/4 c.	water

Have ready:	1 lb.	cottage cheese
	3/4 lb.	cheddar or other cheese
	some	lasagna noodles

Layer twice in 9x13" pan:
sm. amt. sauce
1/2 of lasagna noodles to cover sauce
1/2 of sauce
1/2 of cottage cheese
1/2 of cheddar cheese

Cover with foil. Bake at 350F for 1-1/2 hrs. Let stand
1/2 hr. before serving.

Quick Stroganoff

Sauté:	1 lb.	ground beef
	1 sm.	onion, chopped
	1 clove	garlic, chopped
	4 oz.	mushrooms, sliced

Add, bring to boil: 2 T.   flour   1 t.   salt
                    1/4 t. pepper

Add, simmer 10 min: 1 can   cream of chicken soup

Add and heat through: 1 c. sour cream or mock sour cream
                      or plain yogurt

Serve over cooked noodles with buttered squash and tossed
salad.

Mock Sour Cream

1/3 c.	buttermilk	1 T.	lemon juice
8 oz.	cottage cheese		

Blend in processor or blender until liquified and smooth.
Refrigerate several hours or overnite to chill and
thicken. Add minced chives before serving as a potato
topping.

Spaghetti Sauce

Brown: 1-1/2 lb. hamburger
        1 lg.   onion, chopped
        1 clove garlic, chopped

Add: 1 can   tomatoes (1g.)(Or 1 qt. home processed)
        1 can   tomato soup
        1 can   tomato sauce (8 oz.)
        1 can   tomato paste (8 oz.)
        1 T.   sugar (optional)
        1   bay leaf
        1 t.   salt
        1/4 t. pepper
        1/4 t. thyme
        1/2 t. oregano
        1/2 t. basil

Simmer 1 hr. Serve over 1 lb. whole wheat or regular
spaghetti.

Spanish Beef-Rice

Brown: 1 lb.   ground beef
        1 lg.   onion, chopped
        1 sm.   green pepper, chopped
        1 c.   raw rice

Add: 1 t.   salt
        2 t.   mustard
        1 qt.   canned tomatoes

Simmer, covered, 30 min., longer if using brown rice.

Chow Mein

Brown: 1 lb.   fresh pork steaks, cubed
          1 c.   onion, diced
          1 c.   mushrooms, sliced

Add and simmer 15 min. or 'til meat is tender:
2 c.   celery, sliced
2 c.   chicken stock (or water and bouillon)
2 T.   soy sauce
1 t.   salt

Stir in and cook 'til thickened:
3 T.   cornstarch moistened with water

Serve over rice, chow mein noodles, or toast points. May substitute ground beef for pork.

Chinese Hamburger Hash

Brown: 1-1/2 lb. ground beef
          2 lg.   onions, chopped
          2 c.   celery, chopped

Add in lg. pot: 1 can   cream of mushroom soup
                  1 can   cream of chicken soup
                  4 c.   water
                  2 c.   brown rice, raw
                  1/4 c. soy sauce

Bake at least 1 hr. at 350F. Uncover last half of cooking time.

Bean Sprout Dish

Brown: 1 lb. ground beef   1   onion, chopped

Stir in and heat:
1/2 t.   salt   ]
1/4 t.   pepper   ]
2 T.   soy sauce   ] Bake for
1 can   cream of mushroom soup] 1 hr. at
1 can   cream of chicken soup   ] 350F.
1 can   water   ]
3/4 c.   raw rice   ]
16 oz.   bean sprouts, fresh or canned (drained)]

Oriental Skillet Supper

Stir-fry 'til crisp-tender: 1 c.   green pepper strips
                                   2/3 c. celery
                                   2 T.   oil

Remove above and brown quickly: 2 lg. minute steaks, in strips (excellent use for your doggie-bag steaks)

Stir together and add, stirring 'til thickened:
2/3 c. cold water   2 T.   soy sauce
4 t.   cornstarch   1 t.   sugar
1/2 t.   salt

Add with cooked vegetables: 2 med. tomatoes, cut in wedges

Heat through and serve over 2 c. hot cooked rice tossed with 1/2 t. ginger. Good with orange or mandarin orange salad.

Pork Chops and Rice

Brown and season: 6 pork chops or steaks

Layer in casserole: 1-1/2 c. rice
                         the   chops, browned
                         1 slice onion per chop
                         1 qt.   tomatoes
                         2 c.   beef broth or bouillon

Bake for 45 min. covered, 15 min. uncovered at 300F. (Longer with brown rice.)

NOTES:

Seven Layer Casserole

1 c.	raw rice
1 c.	canned corn, drained
some	salt and pepper
1 can	tomato sauce (8 oz.)
1/2 can	water
1/2 c.	onion, chopped
1/2 c.	green pepper
3/4 lb.	uncooked ground beef (chuck is best, since you can't drain it)
1 can	tomato sauce
1/2 can	water
4 strips bacon	

Place in 2 qt. casserole in order given. Bake at 350F for 1 hr. covered, 1/2 hr. uncovered or 'til bacon is crisp.

Baked Brown Rice Curry

1/2 c.	butter
1 lg.	onion, chopped
1 clove	garlic, chopped
1-1/2 c.	brown rice
2 cans	chicken broth (13-1/2 oz. each) (Or equivalent in bouillon)
1/2 c.	parsley, chopped
2	tomatoes, chopped
1 t.	salt
1/4 t.	pepper
1/2 t.	curry

Stir ingredients together in 9x13" pan. Cover with foil and bake at 350F for 1 hr. Remove foil and bake 30 min. more. Fluff with fork before serving.

Oostbury Dish

Layer in casserole:

some	raw potato, sliced	]
some	onion, chopped	] Bake for
some	beef or hamburger, chopped	] 1 hr. at
1 can	baked beans	] 350F.
1 can	tomato soup	]

Millie's Chow Mein

Brown: 1 lb.   hamburger
           1 lb.   sausage
           some   onion
           some   celery

Add and cook 'til tender: some   carrots, diced
                                   some   potatoes, diced

Add and heat through: some   peas

Hamburger Potato Hotdish

Layer in dish: some   potato, sliced
                   some   raw hamburger, crumbled
                 1 can   vegetable soup
                 1 can   mushroom soup

Season. Bake at 350F for 1-1/2 hrs.

Hamburger Hotpot

Brown: 1 lb.   hamburger
           some   garlic

Layer in dish: 6   potatoes, sliced
                   some   onion, chopped
                             browned hamburger
                 1 can   mushroom soup
                 dribble milk

Bake covered for 1-1/2 hrs. at 350F.

Six Layer Dinner

Layer: 2 c.   raw potatoes, sliced
         2 c.   celery, chopped
         1 lb.   raw hamburger, crumbled
         1/2 c.   onion, sliced
         1-1/2 t. salt
         1/4 t.   pepper
         1 can   tomato soup
         some   green pepper, chopped

Bake covered at 350F for 2 hrs.

Oven Stew

Layer in casserole: 3 lb.   stew meat   ] Bake at
                   2 cans mushroom soup] 300F for
                   1 pkg. onion soup   ] about 5 hrs.

Cedric's Casserole

Brown: 1 lb.   ground beef
        1   onion, chopped
        3/4 t.   salt
        1/8 t.   pepper

Shred: 1/2 head cabbage

Spread half of cabbage in 3 qt. dish; cover with meat; then remaining cabbage. Spread 1 can tomato soup over all. Bake at 350F for 1 hr. Bake potatoes alongside for a complete meal.

For a very hurried supper, cook in covered pan on top of stove for 1/2 hr. or 'til very tender. Serve with fried potatoes.

Joan's Hearty Hotdish

Cook in salted water: 2   onions, chopped
                         3   carrots, sliced
                         3 stalks celery, sliced

Add: 1-1/2 lb. hamburger, browned
      1 pkg.   frozen green limas
      2 cans   tomatoes (16 oz. each)
      1/4 c.   catsup
      2 T.   vinegar
      2 t.   mustard
      some   salt and pepper

Bake in casserole for 1 hr. at 325F.

250

Chili For A Crowd (or to freeze)

Prepare according to pkg. directions:
1 lb. pkg. dry pinto or kidney beans

Brown in dutch oven:

3 lbs.	hamburger
3	onions, chopped
3 cloves	garlic, chopped
1 lg.	green pepper, chopped

Add:

1-1/2 qt.	canned tomatoes (or fresh)
1 T.	salt
1 T.	Worcestershire sauce
some	chili powder to taste

Cover and simmer 1 hr. covered. Add prepared pinto beans and cook 1 more hr., uncovered.

Baked Beans in Cider

Wash and soak 12 hrs: 4 c. dried beans—cold water to cover

Add to drained beans and boil 1/2 hr:
1 bottle semi-sweet cider

Layer in bean pot:

1/2 lb.	salt pork (save some for top)
1 lg.	onion, chopped
the	beans and cider
some	dry mustard
1/2 c.	molasses
reserved	salt pork
some	hot water to cover
some	salt

Cover and bake for 4 to 6 hrs. in slow oven. Uncover for last hr. and add water if beans are too dry. May use meaty ham bone instead of salt pork.

My Favorite Recipe _____

MEATS

My Favorite Recipe _____

Special Beef Stew

Brown: 1-1/2 lb. round steak, in 1" cubes
      3 T.   flour
      2 T.   butter
      1 clove garlic, minced

Add: 1 pkg.   dry onion soup

Add and cook 45 min: 1 c.   water
                          1/2 c.   red wine
                          1   bay leaf

Add and cook 20 min: 2 c.   carrots, sliced
                          1 can   mushrooms

Serve over mashed potatoes. Serves 4 to 6.

Delores' Swiss Steak

Pound round steak with flour, salt, and pepper. Brown.
Add 1/2 can tomato sauce and pan juices. Bake 1 hr. Add
carrots, potatoes, onions, and other 1/2 can tomato sauce.
Bake 1 hr. longer.

Swiss Bliss

Layer in dish:
2 lbs.   chuck steak, cut in serving pieces
1 pkg.   onion soup
1/2 lb. mushrooms, sliced
1/2   green pepper, sliced
1 lb.   tomatoes, drained and chopped (canned)
some   pepper

Combine: 1/2 c. juice from tomatoes
         1 T.   A-1 steak sauce
         1 T.   cornstarch

Pour sauce over everything is dish. Cover tightly, bake 2
hrs. at 375F. Add baked potatoes and a baked vegetable
dish alongside last hr.

Pot Roast

Put roast in pan. Sprinkle with 1 pkg. dry onion soup. Cover and bake at 200F-250F for 3 -4 hrs. Add potatoes, carrots, and onions 1-1/2 hrs. before serving. One pan to clean!

Stove-Top Pork Chop Supper

Brown:	4	pork chops or steaks]	
		]	
Add:	1 can	tomato soup	] Cover;
	1/2 c.	water	] simmer for
	1 t.	Worcestershire	] 45 min. or
	1/2 t.	salt	] 'til tender.
	1/2 t.	caraway or oregano	]
	4	potatoes, quartered	]
	4	carrots, in chunks	]

Pork Stir-Fry

Brown: 1/2 lb.   fresh pork, in strips] Push meat
          2 T.   oil   ] to side.

Add and stir-fry 2 min: 1/2 lb. broccoli, sliced
                        1/2 lb. mushrooms, sliced
                        1/2 c.   green onions, chopped

Combine: 1/4 c.   water
         2 T.   soy sauce
         1 T.   dry cooking sherry
         1 T.   honey
         1 t.   cornstarch
         1/2 t.   Accent
         1/8 t.   garlic powder

Add and heat 'til sauce begins to thicken. Stir in and heat: 1 can Mandarin oranges, drained. Serve immediately over 2 c. cooked hot rice.

Karen's Swedish Meatballs

1-1/2 lb. ground beef
1   onion, minced
1-2   eggs
1/2 c.   flour
1 t.   salt or celery salt
some   pepper
3/4 c.   milk (approx.)

Mix together. Form with t. and brown in butter. Drain
off fat and add 1 can mushroom soup with 3/4 can milk for
gravy. Serve over boiled potatoes.

Hamburger Pizza

1-1/2 lb. hamburger   1   egg, beaten
1 t.   salt   1/8 t. pepper
1/4 t. garlic powder   1/4 c. onion, chopped
1/2 can tomato sauce

Mix. Pat lightly into greased 10" pie plate. Bake 15
min. at 400F. Pour off juices.

Spread over top: 1/2 can   tomato sauce
                   1/4 t.   oregano
                   some   Mozzarella cheese, slices

Broil 7 min. or 'til bubbly. Serves 6.

Delores' BBQ's

Brown: 2-1/2 lbs. hamburger, onion, and celery.

Add: 1 can   tomato soup
         1-1/2 T. Worcestershire
         1 T.   lemon juice
         1 T.   brown sugar
         1/2 t.   salt
         1/4 t.   pepper
         some   ketchup (optional)

Simmer 30 min.

Speedy BBQ's

Brown: 1 lb. hamburger

Add: 1 can tomato sauce
      some salt and pepper
      some bottled BBQ sauce to taste

Simmer to blend flavors and serve.

Sloppy Joe's

Brown: 1 lb. ground beef

Add: 1 can chicken gumbo soup
      some mustard
      some salt and pepper

Heat through and serve.

Hamburger French Bread

Brown: 1-1/2 lb. hamburger
        1   onion, chopped
        3/4 t.   oregano
        1/2 t.   salt
        1/4 t.   pepper

Hollow out: 1 loaf French bread

Add to meat: the   French bread crumbs
              1   egg, slightly beaten
              1/4 t.   dry mustard
              1-1/2 c.   cheddar cheese, shredded

Mix well. Fill hollowed out French bread. Wrap in foil
Bake for 15 to 20 min.

Hamburger Big Boys

Mix together:

1-1/2 lb.	ground chuck	
2/3 c.	canned milk	
1	egg, slightly beaten	
1/2 c.	cracker crumbs	
1/2 c.	onion, chopped	
1 T.	mustard	
1-1/2 t.	salt	
1/8 t.	pepper	
1 c.	cheddar cheese, shredded	

Spread on 1 loaf French bread cut in half lengthwise.
Wrap in foil and bake at 350F for 30 to 45 min.

Dottie's Hot Beef

2	beef roasts
1	pork roast
some	garlic salt
2-3 cans	chicken broth

Bake covered 5 to 6 hrs. at low temperature. Using 2
forks shred and pull the meat apart. It will soak up all
the juices. Remove any fat or membrane. Serve hot on
buns. Serves a huge crowd, and leftovers are great to
package in meal-size portions to freeze.

NOTES:

My Favorite Recipe _____

POULTRY

My Favorite Recipe _____

POULTRY

Tarragon Chicken

Place chicken pieces in single layer in shallow roasting
pan; sprinkle with onion salt and tarragon; bake at 350F
for 1 hr. Baste with pan juices after 15 min., and again
a little later if you think of it. Use pan juices for
gravy, or save for cooking rice, etc. another day. (For
extra-easy meal bake potatoes alongside chicken.)

Oven Chicken

Melt: 1 stick butter

Add: 1 T.   salt
          1 T.   sugar
          1 T.   mustard

Pour over chicken. Bake for 2 hrs. at 350F. Enough for 2
chickens.

Easy Glazed Chicken

Mix: lemon juice concentrate
          mayonnaise
          Parmesan cheese

Roast chicken 'til almost done. Spread mixture on chicken
and bake 10 min. longer.

Imperial Chicken

Combine: 1 c.   bread crumbs
         1/3 c.   Parmesan cheese
         1/8 c.   parsley, chopped
         some   garlic powder
         some   salt and pepper

Dip chicken in oil, then crumbs. Bake 1 hr. at 350F.

Yorkshire Chicken

Bake 1 cut-up fryer or other chicken pieces in shallow roasting pan for 40 min. at 400F. (season with salt, pepper, and sage.) Prepare Yorkshire Pudding, pour over chicken, and bake for 20 to 25 min. longer until puffed and brown.

Yorkshire Pudding—

Sift: 1 c.   flour
          1 t.   baking powder
          1 t.   salt

Gradually beat in: 3   eggs
                 1-1/2 c. milk
                 1 T.   dried parsley

Baked Chicken with Vegetables

Place in lg. roasting pan: 4   potatoes, cut up
                            6   carrots, cut up
                            2 lg.   onions, quartered

Cover with: 1   chicken, cut up

Mix: 1/2 c. hot water   1 t.   thyme
    1 t.   salt   1/4 t. pepper

Spoon over chicken and vegetables. Bake at 400F for 1 hr. or more, until browned and tender. Baste with pan drippings once or twice during cooking. Pop Quick Oil Biscuits in oven last 15 min., and serve with Banana Cole Slaw.

NOTES:

Quick Microwave Chicken

Place in baking dish: 1 chicken, cut up

Season with: 1 t.   salt   1 t.   paprika
             1/2 t. rosemary

Add on top: 4   potatoes, cut up
            6   carrots, cut up
            2   onions, quartered

Cover with plastic wrap. Microwave on high 15 min. Stir and turn the dish, cover and cook 10 min. longer. Let stand 5 to 7 min. before serving.

Turkey Loaf

1 lb.   turkey, ground and uncooked
1   egg, beaten
1/2 c.   milk
2 slices bread, crumbled
some   onion, green pepper, celery, chopped
1/2 t.   basil
1 t.   poultry seasoning
some   pepper
1 T.   bacon fat or butter

Combine ingredients. Bake in loaf pan at 325F for 1 hr. Bake potatoes and Broccoli Puff along with meat loaf for a complete oven meal.

Blender hint: Crumb bread slices in blender. Remove. Blend together milk, egg, chunked vegetables, seasoning and fat. Add all to turkey and mix.

Food processor: First chop vegetables, then add bread and process, then remaining ingredients and process lightly.

Turkey-Dressing Loaf: Make approximately 1/2 recipe dressing (next page) using maximum amount of butter. Mound it firmly in roasting or cake pan and cover with turkey mixture. Slice in wedges to serve.

Mother's Poultry Dressing

Cube day ahead and allow to dry in open bowl:
1 loaf   day old bread

Sauté: 1 to 1-1/2 sticks of butter
          4 stalks celery
          1   onion
          4 T.   parsley

Add: 1 chicken bouillon cube

Add to bread with vegetables and toss:
1 T.   sage   1 t.   salt
1/4 t. pepper

Beat together, pour over cubes, and toss: 2   eggs
                                           3 T.   water

Enough stuffing for 2 roasting chickens or ducks or 1 turkey.

Chicken with Brown Rice

Sprinkle in bottom of roasting pan or dish:
1 pkg.   onion soup

Sprinkle on top: 1 c. brown rice

Arrange on rice: 1 fryer, cut up, salted

Mix: 1 can   mushroom or chicken soup
          1-1/2 c. water

Pour soup over chicken. Cover pan. Bake at 350F for 1-1/2 to 2 hrs. Uncover last half hr. Bake squash or Sweet Potato Puff alongside.

If you're doubling it, you can increase everything but the soups and it's still great. (You may want to for planned-overs.) You can eliminate the mushroom or chicken soup altogether if you don't happen to have any on the shelf, as the chicken drippings provide much of the flavor. In that case, just use 2 c. water to every cup of rice. You can bake it at 250F for 4 hrs. if you're going out and want dinner ready when you get home.

Broccoli Chicken Rice Casserole

Layer in this order:

	2 c.	cooked brown rice
	1 bunch	broccoli, slighly cooked
	2 c.	cooked chicken, cubed

Combine:

	1 can	chicken or mushroom soup
	1/2 c.	mayonnaise
	1/2 c.	milk
	1 T.	lemon juice
	1/2 t.	curry

Spread on top. Add grated cheese, if desired. Bake at 350F for 1/2 hr. or so, or warm in microwave at 1/2 powder 'til heated through.

Karen's Turkey Broccoli Dish

Layer 1: cooked cut-up broccoli

Layer 2: cooked cut-up turkey (or chicken)

Layer 3, combine:

1 can	chicken, celery or mushroom soup
1/2-1 c.	mayonnaise (depending on amount of chicken and broccoli)
1 T.	lemon juice
1/4 t.	curry

Spread over turkey. Bake in oven or microwave 'til hot. Good over rice or baked potatoes.

NOTES:

Family Casserole

```
1-1/2 to
2 c.       rice, cooked
2 c.       chicken or turkey, cooked and diced
1 sm.      onion, diced
1/2-1      green pepper, in strips
3 stalks   celery, in diagonal thin slices
1 sm.can   mushrooms (or fresh)
1 can      mushroom soup
some       salt and pepper
3/4 c.     cheese, grated
1/3 c.     toasted almonds, slivered (optional)
```

Layer everything but cheese twice in wide casserole.
Sprinkle with cheese and almonds. Bake, covered, at 350F
for 30 min. or 'til heated through.

Microwave: 10 min. on high, turning half way through; then
20 min. or so on med.

Chicken with Rice and Raisins

Combine in roasting or baking pan:
```
1 c.       rice, uncooked
1 med.     onion, chopped
1/2 c.     raisins
1/2 t.     garlic salt
1/2 t.     seasoned salt
1/2 t.     oregano
1 t.       paprika
1 lb.      canned stewed or plain tomatoes
1-1/2 c.   water
```

Add on top: 3 lbs. chicken pieces, raw, browned if
desired.

Cover and bake at 400F for about 1 hr., uncovering last 15
min. or so to brown chicken.

Easy Chinese Chicken

Combine and heat:
1 can		celery soup
4 oz.		mushrooms, including juice
1 can		water chestnuts
1 c.		chicken, cubed
1 T.		soy sauce

Serve on: 3 c.   rice, cooked

(Broccoli stems can be used for crunchy texture in place of water chestnuts, if peeled, sliced, and added just before serving. May also be served over toast points, chinese noodles, popovers, cooked noodles, cornbread, or whatever suits your time or imagination.)

Quick Chicken Stir-Fry

Stir-fry 'til crisp-tender:
2 T.   oil
1 c.   broccoli flowerets
1 c.   cauliflowerets
3/4 c.   carrots, sliced diagonal
1/4 c.   green onion, slices
1 clove   garlic, minced

Add and heat: 2 c.   leftover chicken chunks

Remove from heat and add: 1/2 c.   salad dressing
                             1 T.   soy sauce
                             1/2 t.   ginger

Serve with parsley-buttered rice or rice cooked in chicken broth along-side, if desired.   Serves 4.   Also good served in hot, split popovers.

NOTES:

Chicken Divan

Layer in dish: cooked broccoli
chicken or ham, sliced

Combine:
2 c.	white sauce
1/2 c.	cheese, shredded
some	onion, grated
2 t.	mustard
1 t.	salt

Stir sauce 'til cheese melts. Pour over meat and vegetables. Bake at 400F for 25 to 30 min.

Chow Ki Tau

Stir-fry 'til cooked: chicken breast strips
(or use leftover chicken)

Remove and add: celery, sliced diagonally

Stir in and simmer 3 min: snow peas, almonds or water chestnuts, chicken, and chicken broth with 1 t. cornstarch added per c.

Serve with stir-fried rice.

Sprout Stir-Fry

Mix: 2 T.   soy sauce
     1/2 t. sugar

Have ready: 2 raw chicken breasts, in strips
(or 2 c. cooked turkey or chicken)
2 c. mung-bean or lentil sprouts
1 green pepper, in strips
1 lg. stalk celery, in diagonal slices

Heat 2 T. oil in heavy skillet. Add chicken and cook, stirring, 2 min. on med.-high. Add vegetables and stir-fry 1 min. Add soy sauce, stir and cook 1 min. Serve immediately. Makes 4 servings.

Scalloped Chicken

Heat and stir: 1 can   mushroom soup
               1 c.   milk

Toss together:
4-6 c.   dried bread crumbs
1/2 c.   butter, melted
some   sage, thyme, onion salt, garlic salt, and parsley

Have ready: 2 c.   chicken, cooked and diced

Arrange layers of chicken, soup, and crumbs. Top with grated cheese, if desired. Bake at 350F for 25 to 30 min.

Chicken Spaghetti Casserole

Cook: 1 pkg.   spaghetti (8 oz.)

Sauté: 1 c.   mushrooms
        1/4 c.   onion
        1/4 c.   green pepper
        1/2 c.   celery
        1 clove garlic, minced

Add: 1 can   tomatoes
        1/4 c.   olives (optional)

Add: 1 whole chicken, cooked and boned (or leftovers)
        some   spaghetti, cooked

Turn into shallow baking dish. Cover with grated cheese and heat for 20 to 30 min. Can be made a day ahead and tastes even better if it sets awhile before heating.

NOTES:

271

Chicken Tetrazzini

Make white sauce:
1/4 c.	butter
1/4 c.	flour
1 t.	salt
1/4 t.	garlic salt
1/8 t.	pepper
2 c.	milk
2 c.	half & half (or milk)
2	chicken bouillon cubes

Add:
1/3 c.	sherry
2/3 c.	Parmesan
1/3 c.	white cheese, grated

Layer in 9x13" pan:
7 oz.	spaghetti, cooked
2 c.	chicken
3 oz.	mushrooms
the	white sauce
1/3 c.	more white cheese, grated

Bake at 375F for 20 to 30 min. Serve with garlic bread and a tossed salad. Good company meal.

Chicken Macaroni Casserole

Mix:
1 c.	chicken, diced
1 c.	celery, diced
1 c.	uncooked macaroni
1 can	mushroom soup
1 c.	milk
1/8 lb.	Velveeta or other soft cheese
1/2 t.	salt
1/4 t.	thyme

Let stand in refrigerator overnite. Bake at 350F for 45 to 60 min.

Chicken Macaroni Salad

2 c.	cooked macaroni	] Combine
2 c.	chicken, cubed	] and
1 c.	cheese, cubed	] refrigerate
1 lg.	cucumber, peeled and chopped	] until
2	apples, peeled and chopped	] serving
3	tomatoes, chopped	] time.
1 c.	mayonnaise	]
1 t.	salt (include onion and celery salt)	]
1/4-1/2 t.	curry	]

272

Chicken Mushroom Spaghetti Salad

6 oz.	spaghetti, cooked	] Combine and
1-1/2 c.	mayonnaise	] chill several
1 t.	dry mustard (may want less)	] hrs. or
1 t.	salt	] overnite
2 c.	chicken, cubed	] before
1-1/2 c.	halved red seedless grapes	] serving.
1 c.	celery, sliced	]
1/2 c.	green pepper, chopped	]
4 oz.	mushrooms, drained	]

Oriental Chicken Salad

8 oz.	thin spaghetti, cooked	]
2	carrots, in strips, cooked with spaghetti last 5 min.	]
2 T.	sesame seeds, toasted (stir 'til brown in sm. pan)	] Combine
1/2 c.	soy sauce (add to pan with seasonings, below)	] and] chill.
1/3 c.	oil	]
1 T.	sugar	] Good for
1 t.	ginger	] picnics
1 T.	vinegar	] because
2 T.	peanut butter	] there's no
1/4 t.	crushed red pepper	] mayonnaise.
2-1/2 c.	leftover chicken, slivered	]
1/2 c.	green onion, slivered	]

Chicken Fruit Salad

4 c.	leftover chicken, slivered
1 c.	celery, chopped
1 c.	seedless green grapes, halved and/or Mandarin oranges
1 pkg.	toasted almonds, slivered
1 t.	salt
1/4 t.	pepper
1/4 c.	mayonnaise
1/4 c.	sour cream

Combine, chill, and serve on bed of lettuce leaves.

273

Peach and Chicken Cups

Combine: 1/2 c.   sour cream
         1/4 c.   mayonnaise
         1/4 t.   thyme
         1/4 t.   basil
         dash   each sugar, salt and pepper

Add: 2 c.   (or more) leftover chicken, slivered
        1 c.   (or more) peaches, drained and diced
             (celery, if desired)

Chill and Serve.

Chicken Rice Salad

4 c.   cooked chicken
4 T.   stuffed olives, chopped (optional)
1-1/2 c.   celery, chopped
1 t.   pickle relish
4   hard-cooked eggs, sliced
2 c.   cooked rice
1 c.   almonds, slivered
4 T.   ripe olives, chopped

Mix all together. Coat with dressing.

Dressing: Make a dressing using Miracle Whip thinned with some milk, 1 T. white vinegar, 1 t. sugar, and salt and pepper to taste. Use enough salad dressing to coat the salad well.

Chicken Luncheon Sandwich

1-1/2 c.   cooked chicken, diced
1 c.   cheddar cheese, shredded
1/2 c.   celery, finely chopped
1/4 c.   green pepper, chopped
1   green onion, chopped
1 T.   pimento, chopped (optional)
1/2 c.   mayonnaise
1/2 c.   plain yogurt
some   salt and pepper

Combine. Refrigerate 'til ready to use.

SALADS

My Favorite Recipe _____

SALADS

Salads add so much to meals, not only nutritionally, but the variety, texture, and color they offer. Make them ahead of time if possible, to eliminate the last minute pressure when everyone's tired and hungry. It's really nice to pull a salad out of the refrigerator to add to a quick supper. The easiest salad I know is made with alfalfa sprouts. Make a nest of sprouts on each plate and top with chopped tomato, cucumber, broccoli, sliced orange, grapefruit, whatever's on hand, and sprinkle with Italian dressing. Sprouts are expensive in the store, but so easy to grow on your window ledge. I have a batch going all the time. Buy a sprouting jar and seeds at a health food store, and the simple directions will get you started. (Once they're grown and before storing in the refrigerator, I rinse in large bowl in several waters to let the brown seeds run off, then spin dry in salad spinner, and store in plastic bag.) Sprouts are also great in sandwiches because they don't wilt by lunchtime. (Try a cheese, mushroom, and sprout sandwich with a bit of mayonnaise on whole wheat bread for a low calorie lunchbox feast.)

Broccoli is so nutritious that it should be served often. Many children prefer it raw, and the following broccoli salads are easy and delicious. You may want to double the recipes to have on hand for easy week-end suppers.

Broccoli – Pea Salad

Combine: 10 oz. broccoli
10 oz. frozen peas, thawed and drained
3 stalks celery, sliced
1 sm. onion, chopped

Combine and fold into above: 2/3 c. mayonnaise
1/3 c. sour cream
some salt and pepper

Chill. May add 3 hard-boiled eggs before serving.

Raw Cauliflower Salad

Combine: 1 head   cauliflower, sliced
        1 sm.   onion, grated
        3 ribs   celery, sliced thin
        1 pkg.   frozen peas, thawed and drained
        1   green pepper, chopped fine

Combine: 1 c.   Miracle Whip
        3-4 T.   milk (buttermilk is good)
        1 t.   sugar
        1/4 t.   seasoned salt
        1/4 t.   pepper

Mix and refrigerate several hrs. or overnight.

Layered salads take the last minute pressure off suppers as they can be made ahead and tossed just before serving.

Pat's Layered salad

Layer: some   lettuce
        some   frozen peas, uncooked

Spread over top: some   mayonnaise

Top with: 1 t.   sugar (optional)
         some   cheese, cubed
         some   red onion, chopped (may use cooking
                   onions, but use less as it's stronger)

Refrigerate overnite. Toss before serving. (You may be creative with this salad and add anything you have on hand that your family likes...mushrooms, celery, alfalfa sprouts, broccoli, etc.)

NOTES:

Special Salad

Layer in large
glass bowl:

1 head	lettuce, shredded
1	tomato, sliced
1	cucumber, sliced
2	carrots, sliced
3	green onions, chopped
1 c.	fresh mushroom, sliced
1 c.	bean sprouts
1 c.	alfalfa sprouts
1	green pepper, sliced
1 can	black olives, sliced (4 oz.)

Sprinkle over all: 1 T.   oregano

Combine in jar:

1 c.	red wine vinegar
3/4 c.	light soy sauce
1/4 c.	lemon juice
1 t.	pepper
1 T.	Parmesan Cheese

Shake dressing well. Refrigerate 1 hr. before tossing with salad. Again, use your imagination with salad ingredients.

This layered salad is a meal, especially good in summer using leftover grilled chicken, and served with Blueberry Corn Muffins and iced tea.

Chicken Curry Salad

Layer in pretty, glass bowl:
some	salad greens
some	cooked chicken, cut-up
some	frozen peas, drained
some	cucumbers, sliced
some	tomato, chopped

Combine:
3 c.	mayonnaise (depending on how lg. your bowl)
1 T.	sugar
1 t.	curry

Spread over top of salad, sealing to edges. Refrigerate several hrs. or overnite. Garnish with croutons before serving. May also use ham or any other left-over meat.

Salad Croutons

Cube day-old bread or buns. Drizzle with melted butter. Sprinkle with onion and garlic salt or powder and oregano. Toast in low oven 'til browned, stirring occasionally. Store in covered jar for use on salads.

Bacon and Broccoli Salad

Combine:
8 c.	broccoli, sliced (use stems, but if they're thick and tough peel them first)
1/4 c.	onion, chopped
1/2 lb.	bacon, cut up, fried, and drained
2 c.	raisins

Combine:
1/4 c.	sugar (may use less)
1-1/2 c.	mayonnaise
3 T.	cider vinegar

Fold dressing into broccoli and refrigerate 'til serving.

This is a great company salad as it is delicious and can be made a day ahead. Bacon should not be served on a regular basis because of its high cholesterol and nitrate count, but is fine for special occasions.

Ham and Broccoli Macaroni Salad

Combine:
1/2 c.	mayonnaise
2 T.	Parmesan, grated
1 T.	white vinegar
1/16 t.	pepper

Toss in:
1 c.	shell macaroni, cooked and drained
1 c.	broccoli flowerets, cooked and drained
1 c.	julienne strips cooked ham

Refrigerate several hrs. to blend flavors. (Don't throw broccoli stems away. Peel if they're tough and use in a tossed salad another night, or eat for a delicious snack.)

Orange-Almond Salad

Combine in jar:
1/4 c.	salad oil
2 T.	sugar
2 T.	vinegar
1/4 t.	salt
1/8 t.	almond extract

Shake well and chill 'til serving time.

Combine in lg. salad bowl:
6 c. torn mixed greens
3 oranges, peeled, sliced crosswise and halved
1 c. celery, thinly sliced
2 T. green onion, sliced

Sprinkle on: 1/3 c. toasted slivered almonds

Toss with dressing and serve at once. Especially good with duck or any poultry meal.

Easy Orange Lettuce Salad

lettuce
mandarin oranges, drained
almonds, slivered
Wishbone Italian dressing

Toss together and serve.

Summer Fruit Salad

Line shallow salad bowl with: salad greens

Cut in strips and add: 1 avocado

Sprinkle on: 2 T. lemon juice (save some avocado for garnish)

Combine and add:
3 c. cantaloupe balls
1 c. fresh pineapple cubes
1 c. hulled strawberries

Garnish with: 8 oz. cheddar cheese, cut in strips and the remainder of avocado

Serve with Honey-Nut dressing:
1 c. mayonnaise   2 T. honey
2 T. almonds, slivered

Pinwheel Oranges

Slice one peeled orange per person very thin and arrange pinwheel fashion on salad plate. Sprinkle with cinnamon and sugar. Good brunch salad.

Orange-Avocado Salad

2   oranges, peeled and cut in pieces
1   avocado, peeled and cut in pieces
2 T.   vinegar
1-1/2 t.   oil
1/4 t.   salt   1/8 t.   pepper

Toss together in small bowl. Good accompaniment for tacos or any Mexican dish.

Mandarin Orange Salad

2 cans   mandarin oranges, drained
1 c.   celery, sliced
1/4 c.   coconut
2 T.   creamy fruit and slaw dressing
           (or sour cream or mayonnaise)

Toss together; chill and serve in lettuce cups.

The quickest, easiest salad dressing is to thin mayonnaise with milk, buttermilk, fruit juice, tomato juice, pickle juice, etc. When thinned with milk it can be sparked up with a dash of vinegar and a bit of sugar, if you don't object to the sugar. I use sugar in moderation as it offers empty calories with no nutrients. Following are some make-ahead salad dressings that are far cheaper than commercial ones.

Spicy French Dressing

1 c.   salad oil   ]
1/3 c.   vinegar   ]
2 T.   catsup   ] Shake together
1 T.   lemon juice   ] in jar and
1 t.   salt   ] store in refrigerator.
1/2 t.   paprika   ]
1/4 t.   sugar   ]
1/4 t.   pepper   ]

Oil Dressing

Cook 'til thick,
stirring constantly:

1 c.	water
1/3 c.	flour
1 T.	butter

Combine in bowl:

2	egg yolks
1 t.	salt
1 t.	mustard
1/8 t.	red pepper
2 T.	vinegar
2 T.	lemon juice
1 c.	oil

Add cooked mixture and beat together. Cool and store in refrigerator.

Roquefort Dressing

3 oz.	Roquefort cheese
2 c.	mayonnaise
1/2 t.	pepper
1/4 t.	garlic powder
1 c.	buttermilk
1 c.	sour cream
1 t.	Worcestershire sauce

Mix thoroughly and store in refrigerator. Not inexpensive, but delicious if you're a Roquefort cheese fan. Blue cheese may be more readily available and works just as well.

Basic Oil and Vinegar Dressing

1 c.	corn oil
1/3 c.	vinegar
1 T.	sugar
1-1/2 t.	salt
1 clove	garlic, split

Combine in jar. Shake well, chill several hrs., then remove garlic and refrigerate 'til needed.
For ZESTY dressing add:

1/2 t.	paprika
1/2 t.	dry mustard
2 T.	catsup
1 T.	lemon juice
1 t.	Worcestershire sauce

(See next page)

For CREAMY dressing add: (omit garlic)
1/4 c.   sugar (total)
1/2 c.   sour cream
1/4 c.   catsup
1/2 t.   paprika

All the strong flavored vegetables such as broccoli, cauliflower, cabbage, etc. are found to be important deterrents of cancer. Many children don't like the tartness of coleslaw, but this naturally sweeter variety has become a favorite of ours. It is especially good with meat and potato dinners.

Banana Coleslaw

Thin mayonnaise with pineapple juice. (A large can frozen in ice cube trays and stored in a plastic bag enables you to always have on hand the small amount needed here.) Fold in shredded cabbage and sliced banana. Raisins can be used in place of or in addition to bananas.

Carrot-Raisin Slaw

1/2 c.   salad dressing, thinned with orange or
         pineapple juice
1 lb.   carrots, grated   1 c.   raisins

Combine ingredients and serve, or refrigerate 'til serving time.

For Carrot-Peanut Salad substitute 1 c. salted peanuts for raisins.

* * *

The following Jell-O recipes have more calories than nutrients, but I've included them anyway because they're quick and delicious for entertaining.

Bonnie's Cran-Raspberry Jello

Combine in blender: 1 can   jellied cranberries
                          1 ctn.   sour cream (16 oz.)
Combine and add to above: 1 lg.pkg. raspberry (jello)
                          2 c.   boiling water
Gel in pretty mold or clear bowl. Good Holiday salad.

284

Cottage Cheese Fruit Salad

1 ctn.	cottage cheese (1 lb.)
1 pkg.	orange Jello, dry (3 oz.)
1 pkg.	Cool Whip (4-1/2 oz.)
1 sm.can	crushed pineapple, drained
1 can	mandarin oranges, drained

Combine all ingredients and refrigerate at least a day before serving. (Any fruit or Jello may be used.)

My Favorite Recipe _____

My Favorite Recipe _____

SOUPS

My Favorite Recipe _____

SOUPS

Bechinalt

Simmer 1 hr.:
1 lb.   chicken gizzards, cleaned well
2-3 t.   salt
3 c.   water

Remove and cut in small pieces.

Sauté:
2 T.   butter
2-3 clv.   garlic

Stir in:
3 T.   flour
1 c.   soup broth from above

Stir flour mixture into broth; add gizzards. Simmer 10 to
15 min. Eat from bowls, dipping fresh bread into broth.

Betty Rae's German Potato Soup

Sauté:
1 lg.   onion, chopped
2 cloves   garlic, minced
3 stalks   celery, sliced

Add:
3-4   potatoes, diced
2 cans   chicken broth (14 oz. each)
           (or equivalent in bouillon)

Simmer 30 min. Whirl 1/3 at a time in blender. Return to
pot and add 1-1/2 c. milk. Reheat, but don't boil.
Season to taste. Serve hot with shredded cheese on top
and seasoned croutons. Delicious!

Tomato Soup From Home Canned Tomatoes

Make white sauce:	3 T.	butter
	3 T.	flour
	2 c.	milk

Heat and add:	1 qt.	tomatoes or tomato juice

Season and serve with grilled cheese sandwiches. A touch of cloves is good.

Easy Split Pea Soup

12 oz.	dried peas
7 c.	water
2 lg.	ham hocks (or bones)
1	onion, chopped
2	bay leaves
12	peppercorns
1/2 t.	salt

Combine in large pot. Boil gently 1 hr. or until peas are soft. Remove ham bones, bay leaves, and peppercorns. Whip peas with wire whisk, if desired, to blend into soup.

Quick Soup

Toss 1 c. leftover spinach, peas, cauliflower, or carrots in blender. Add 1 c. chicken broth, 1/2 c. evaporated milk and blend. Add dash of curry, Worcestershire, if desired. Heat and serve!

Hearty Soup Mix

14 oz.	split peas	]
12 oz.	pearl barley	] Combine and
14 oz.	alphabet macaroni	] store in
12 oz.	lentils	] glass jar.
1-1/2 c.	brown rice	]

Hearty Soup From Mix

Simmer 1-1/2 hrs.: 6 c.   water
                    1-1/3 c. soup mix
                    1-1/2 T. salt

Add. Simmer 1/2 hr.: 1   onion, chopped
                     2   carrots, sliced
                     2 stalks   celery, chopped
                     1-1/2 c.   cabbage, shredded
                     2 cans   tomato sauce (15 oz. each)
                     1 can   vegetable juice cocktail
                                (24 oz.)(or canned tomatoes)
                     1 lb.   meat, cooked - if desired

If you have any meaty bones, they can go in with water and
soup mix. You can also use home canned tomatoes in place
of the tomato sauce if you cut back on the water.

Cream of Onion Soup

Sauté: 2 c.   onion, chopped
           1/2 c.   butter

Blend in: 1/4 c.   flour
           1-1/2 t. salt
           1/4 t.   pepper

Stir in: 4 c.   milk

Bring to a boil, stirring constantly. Boil 1 min.

NOTES:

French Onion Soup

Sauté: 2   onions, thinly sliced
            2 T.   butter

Add and heat:
2 cans   beef broth (14 oz. each)(or bouillon)
1/2 c.   water
1 t.   Worcestershire

Toast: 4 slices French bread

Sprinkle with: Parmesan cheese
Top with: Mozzarella or Monterey Jack cheese

Broil toast in oven or heat in microwave to melt cheese. Ladle soup into 4 serving bowls. Place 1 slice bread in each bowl. Serves 4.

Cheddar Chowder

Cook 'til tender:
2 c.   potatoes, diced   2   carrots, sliced
3/4 c.   onion, chopped   1/2 c.   celery, diced
1/2 c.   water

Melt: 1/4 c.   butter

Blend in:
1/4 c.   flour   1 t.   seasoned salt
1/4 t.   pepper   1/2 t.   dry mustard

Stir in: 1 T.   Worcestershire
         2 c.   milk

When thickened, add: 3/4 c.   cheddar, shredded
                    the   vegetables, cooked

Add and heat: 1 t.   parsley
              1 c.   canned tomatoes, drained

A hearty supper soup. Serves. 4 to 6.

A handful of oatmeal thickens soups.

Thick Barley Chicken Soup

4 c.	water
1 lb.	gizzards, cut up
1/2 c.	barley
1/2 c.	onion, chopped
1	chicken bouillon cube
1 t.	salt
1	bay leaf
1/2 t.	poultry seasoning

Simmer 1 hr. or until gizzards are tender.

NOTES:

My Favorite Recipe _____

VEGETABLES

My Favorite Recipe _____

Piquant Vegetable Stir-Fry

Stir-fry 'til tender-crisp:
2 c.	broccoli, sliced
2	carrots, sliced diagonally
1 clove	garlic, minced
1	onion, in wedges

Stir in:
2 T.	vinegar
2 t.	mustard
some	salt and pepper

Serve immediately. Serves 4. Good accompaniment with fish.

Mushroom Potatoes

1 lb.	fresh mushrooms, sliced or chopped
1 lg.	onion, chopped
3 cloves	garlic, crushed or sliced
2 T.	soy sauce
2 T.	water
6 med.	potatoes, baked

Combine everything but potatoes in lg. skillet and simmer 'til onions are transparent. Serve over potatoes. Serves 6. (Only 141 calories per serving!)

Twice Baked Potatoes

Clean, bake and halve: 6 potatoes

Combine: the	scooped out potato from halves
3 T.	butter
3 T.	mayonnaise
2/3 c.	cottage cheese
1/2 t.	onion salt
some	finely ground pepper

Blend in gradually: 3/4 c. milk
Spoon into shells. (May freeze at this point.) Sprinkle with paprika. Heat through and serve.

Microwave: Microwave unbaked potatoes all together on a plate, 8 min. on each side. Just before serving stuffed potatoes, microwave 5 min. to heat through.

Scalloped Potatoes with Onions

Layer in dish:	4	potatoes, sliced
	1	onion, sliced or chopped
	1/4 c.	flour
	the	salt and pepper

Scald: 1 c. milk. Add 1 T. butter to milk and pour over potatoes. Bake covered for 1 hr. at 300-325F. Uncover and bake 15 min. longer. (May add a layer of crushed soda crackers along with potatoes.) Add chunks of ham in between potato layers for a one-dish meal. Add cubed cheese for cheesy potatoes.

Hot 'N Hearty Potato Salad

Sauté:	1 T.	butter
	1	onion, chopped

Stir in:	1/2 c.	mayonnaise
	1/3 c.	cider vinegar
	1 T.	sugar
	1 t.	salt
	1/4 t.	pepper

Add and heat: 4 potatoes, cooked and sliced (don't boil)

Garnish with:	1 T.	parsley, chopped
	1 T.	bacon, cooked and crumbled

Lettuce Dressing

Sour 1/2 c. cream with 2 T. vinegar and sugar to taste (about 1/2 T.). Toss with tender garden leaf lettuce, and serve over boiled potatoes.

Karen's Potatoes

Melt 1 stick butter in 9x12" pan. Peel potatoes and make slices on each one, not slicing quite through potato. Roll in butter. Bake at 400F for 15 min., then sprinkle with salt, pepper and bread crumbs. Bake for 30 min. or more.

Sweet Potato Whip

Whip cooked sweet potatoes and thin a bit with orange
juice. Add salt, grated orange rind, and a drizzle of
honey, if desired. Put in shallow casserole, dot with
butter, and bake with the rest of your dinner 'til lightly
browned. Good with pork chops and rice casserole.

Golden Sweet Potato Puff

Beat 'til smooth: 3 c. sweet potatoes, cooked (3 lg.)

Beat in: 1/4 c.   butter
        1/3 c.   orange juice

Sauté: 1 T.   butter
      1/3 c.   onion, chopped

Beat into sweet potatoes:
the   onion, sautéd   1/2 t.   salt
1/8 t. pepper   1/4 t.   tarragon
4   egg yolks

Beat 4 egg whites until stiff. Fold egg whites into sweet
potatoes. Bake in greased 1-1/2 qt. dish for 50 min. at
350F, or until puffed and lightly browned.

Thanksgiving Sweet Potatoes

6   sweet potatoes   1/3 c.   brown sugar
1/3 c.   honey or light Karo   1/2 c.   orange juice
1-1/3 T. cornstarch   1 t.   salt
3 T.   butter

Parboil sweet potatoes and cool. Peel and slice
lengthwise 1/2" thick. Combine remaining ingredients in
saucepan and boil 5 min. Pour over potatoes and bake 20
min. at 375F.

Panned Summer Squash

1 qt. squash, sliced   3 T.   butter
1 t.   salt   some   finely ground pepper

Scrub squash and cut in 1/8" slices. Melt butter in
skillet; add squash and season. Cover and cook over med.
heat for 10 to 15 min., turning often to cook evenly.
Shredded cabbage or carrots may be substituted for squash.

Scalloped Corn

1 can	cream style corn
1	egg, well beaten
1 c.	cracker crumbs
3/4 c.	milk
some	celery, sliced thin
some	green pepper, chopped
2 T.	whole wheat or reg. flour

Combine and pour into greased dish. Sprinkle with paprika and dot with butter. Bake at 350F for 30 to 40 min.

Microwave: 50% power 15 to 20 min., turning half way through.

Easy Cauliflower Casserole

Cook: 1 lg. cauliflower, broken into flowerettes

Combine:	1/2 c.	mayonnaise
	1/2 c.	cheddar cheese, shredded
	1/2 t.	dry mustard
	1/4 t.	salt
	1/8 t.	red pepper

Spread sauce over cauliflower in 1 qt. casserole. Bake at 400F for 8 to 10 min. or 'til bubbly. Also good with broccoli.

Scalloped Onions

Separate into rings in dish: 6 onions

Melt: 1/4 c. butter

Blend in: 1/4 c. flour

Stir in; cook 'til thickened: 2 c. milk

| Stir in: | 1/2 t. | salt |
| | 2 c. | cheese, grated |

Pour over onions. Bake uncovered at 375F for 1 hr.

Gingered Carrots

Cook 'til barely tender: 1 lb. carrots, sliced

Add:			
	1/4 t.	ginger	]
	1 t.	sugar or honey	] Stir together
	2 T.	butter	] and serve.
	2 T.	parsley, chopped	]

Carrots and Zucchini

Sauté 'til crisp-tender:	6 med.	zucchini, sliced thin
	6	carrots, sliced thin
	1 T.	butter
	1 T.	oil

Add:	2 T.	honey
	1 T.	lemon juice
	some	salt and pepper

Toss lightly and serve immediately.

Stir-Fry Spinach

Combine:	3 t.	lemon juice
	1-1/2 T.	soy sauce
	1-1/2 t.	sugar

Stir-fry briefly:	1-1/2 c.	celery, diagonal slices
	1 can	mushrooms (or 1 c.)
	1/2 c.	onion, thinly sliced

Add:	6 c.	torn spinach
	and	lemon juice mixture

Cook, stirring quickly, about 2 min. or 'til vegetables are tender-crisp and spinach is just limp. Do not overcook.

Herbed Spinach Bake (or Broccoli)

Cook and drain: 10 oz. spinach or broccoli

Mix with:
1 c.	rice, cooked
1 c.	cheese, shredded
2	eggs, slightly beaten
2 T.	butter, soft
1/3 c.	milk
2 T.	onion, chopped
1/2 T.	Worcestershire
1 t.	salt
1/4 t.	thyme

Bake in 9" square dish at 350F for 20-25 min., or 'til knife comes out clean.

Donna's Spinach Balls

2 pkg.	chopped spinach, cooked and drained (10 oz. each)
1 lg.	onion, chopped fine
4	eggs, beaten
3/4 c.	butter, melted
1/4 t.	pepper
1/2 t.	garlic salt
1 t.	Parmesan cheese
2 c.	herb stuffing mix

Mix all ingredients. Chill several hrs. Roll into walnut sized balls. Bake for 20 min. at 350F.

I use 1 pkg. spinach, 1 stick butter, and 2 c. dried bread crumbs with my own herbs (see poultry dressing recipe.)

Delores' Broccoli Puff

In a 8" dish: 10 oz. fresh or frozen broccoli, cooked and drained

Stir together:
1 can	mushroom soup
1/2 c.	cheese, shredded

Add gradually:
1/4 c.	milk
1/4 c.	mayonnaise
1	egg, beaten

(Continued on next page)

(Continued from last page)

Topping: 1/4 c.   dry bread crumbs
            1 T.   butter, melted

Pour sauce over broccoli. Top with bread crumbs. Bake at 350F for 45 min. 'til lightly browned. Serves 6.

You can double the recipe with 1 can of soup, lay cheese slices over the broccoli rather than grating, and substitute cracker crumbs for the bread if you wish.

Broccoli or Spinach Puff

Cook and drain: 2 pkg.   broccoli, chopped or spinach
                         (10 oz. each) or equivalent fresh

Beat together: 1 c.   Bisquick
                 1 c.   milk
                 2   eggs
                 1/2 t.   salt

Stir in: 1 c.   cheddar cheese, shredded
                 broccoli, cooked

Bake at 325F for 1 hr. or 'til knife comes out clean.

Broccoli Casserole

In dish: 4 c.   broccoli, cooked

On top: 1 c.   celery, sliced

Combine: 1 can   mushroom soup
         3/4 c. sour cream
         sm. jar pimento (optional)
         1/2 t. salt
         1/8 t. pepper
         1/2 c. cheese, grated

Pour sauce over broccoli. Bake at 350F for 30 min.

Double the cheese and serve in split popovers or over toast points for a meatless supper.

303

Jeff's Eggplant Chili

Sauté: 1 med.   eggplant, peeled and diced
              1   green pepper
              1   onion

Sprinkle over: flour

Add: canned tomatoes
             kidney or pinto beans
             salt and pepper
             chili powder
             paprika

Simmer to blend flavors. Serve hot in bowls with grated cheese on each serving.

Meatless Spaghetti (Low Fat)

Simmer 10 min: 1 lg.   onion, diced
               1-1/2 c. fresh mushrooms
               3 cloves garlic, diced
               1/4 c.   water

Add: 1 can   tomatoes (28 oz.)
        1 can   tomato paste (12 oz.)
        1 can   tomato sauce (15 oz.)
        2 t.   dried oregano
        3 T.   soy sauce
        1   bay leaf
        some   pepper to taste

Simmer 2 hrs. Serve over half of a 22 oz. pkg. spinach or whole wheat spaghetti, cooked. Sprinkle with Parmesan cheese, if desired.

Orange Beets

Cook: 2 t.   sugar
        1/2 t.   salt
        1 t.   cornstarch
        1/2 c.   orange juice (or 1 orange
                 squeezed & some rind)

Add cooked, cubed beets. (1 T. butter optional) Grate orange rind on for garnish.

Pickled Beets

Combine: 1 can   beets, sliced and drained (16 oz.)
         1 sm.   onion, sliced thin

Bring to boil: 1/3 c.   vinegar
                 1 T.   sugar
                 1/4 c.   beet liquid

Pour over beets. Chill to serve.

Vegetable Marinade

Parboil vegetables such as carrots, cauliflower, and broccoli. Put in refrigerator dish or plastic bag and cover with bottled Italian dressing. Fresh mushrooms can be added as is or sliced. Marinate overnite or 24 hrs. Remove from marinade and store 'til served.

Great for picnics or to have on hand for week-ends.

My Favorite Recipe _____

My Favorite Recipe _____

Recipe/Topic Index

Recipe/Topic Index

Recipe/Topic Index

Recipe/Topic Index

Recipe/Topic Index

Recipe/Topic Index

Recipe/Topic Index

Recipe/Topic Index

Recipe/Topic Index

Recipe/Topic Index

Recipe/Topic Index

Recipe/Topic Index

Recipe/Topic Index

Recipe/Topic Index

Recipe/Topic Index

Recipe/Topic Index

Recipe/Topic Index

Recipe/Topic Index

Recipe/Topic Index

Recipe/Topic Index